Praise for
From Misery to Ministry

Brian and Leah Foutz have been through the fire and have come forth like gold. God is using them mightily to minister to others who are reeling after the loss of a child.

They have truly turned Misery into Ministry.

—Carole Lewis
National Director, First Place 4 Health

For those thrust into the dark journey upon the death of a child or for those who come along beside them, Brian and Leah expose their hearts to allow others to find hope through God's redeeming love.

—Melinda Ginter
Chapter Leader, The Compassionate Friends—Katy, Texas
www.compassionatefriends-katy.org

from misery *to* ministry

a walk of faith
through the loss
of a loved one

Brian and Leah Foutz

with Janice Havins

Tate Publishing & *Enterprises*

Scripture quotations marked (KJV) are taken from the *Holy Bible, King James Version*, Cambridge, 1769. Used by permission. All rights reserved.

Scripture quotations marked (MSG) are taken from *The Message*. Copyright © 1993, 1994, 1995, 1996, 2000, 2001, 2002. Used by permission of NavPress Publishing Group.

Scripture quotations marked (NASB) are taken from the *New American Standard Bible®*, Copyright © 1960, 1962, 1963, 1968, 1971, 1972, 1973, 1975, 1977, 1995 by The Lockman Foundation. Used by permission.

Scripture quotations marked (NIV) are taken from the *Holy Bible, New International Version®*. NIV®. Copyright© 1973, 1978, 1984 by International Bible Society. Used by permission of Zondervan. All rights reserved.

Scripture quotations marked (NKJV) are taken from the *New King James Version®*. Copyright © 1982 by Thomas Nelson, Inc. Used by permission. All rights reserved.

Scripture quotations marked (NLT) are taken from the *Holy Bible, New Living Translation*, copyright © 1996. Used by permission of Tyndale House Publishers, Inc., Wheaton, Illinois 60189. All rights reserved.

Scripture quotations marked (TLB) are taken from The Living Bible / Kenneth N. Taylor: Tyndale House, © Copyright 1997, 1971 by Tyndale House Publishers, Inc. Used by permission. All rights reserved.

This book is designed to provide accurate and authoritative information with regard to the subject matter covered. This information is given with the understanding that neither the author nor Tate Publishing, LLC is engaged in rendering legal, professional advice. Since the details of your situation are fact dependent, you should additionally seek the services of a competent professional

The opinions expressed by the author are not necessarily those of Tate Publishing, LLC.

Published by Tate Publishing & Enterprises, LLC
127 E. Trade Center Terrace | Mustang, Oklahoma 73064 USA
1.888.361.9473 | www.tatepublishing.com

Tate Publishing is committed to excellence in the publishing industry. The company reflects the philosophy established by the founders, based on Psalm 68:11,
"The Lord gave the word and great was the company of those who published it."

Book design copyright © 2011 by Tate Publishing, LLC. All rights reserved.
Cover design by Rebekah Garibay
Interior design by Chelsea Womble

Published in the United States of America

ISBN: 978-1-61777-177-4
1. Religion, Christian Life, Death, Grief, Bereavement
2. Religion, Christian Life, Family
11.04.21

Bible Scripture References

King James Version (KJV)
The Message (MSG)
New American Standard Bible (NASB)
New International Version (NIV)
New King James Version (NKJV)
New Living Translation (NLT)
The Living Bible (TLB)

Dedication

This book is a gift from God to all the parents who have lost or may lose a child through death. We have walked this path ourselves and have found some wonderful insights that we desire to share with you, the readers. This is not a story about our daughter, Victoria, her murder, and the lurid details of the guilty party's trials. The incident of her death merely fashioned the canvas on which we were able to paint a portrait of how God planted the fruit of His Spirit within us during a time of great mourning.

Whether you are parents who have lost a child or someone who is acquainted or related to a family in grief, this book may give you some practical and useful information on dealing with the shock and pain of loss. We are not experts. We are a family who knows the pain and suffering from a great loss. It is our wish that this book may assuage and validate the grief and the trials you are enduring. Your mourning the passing of a loved one, especially a child who had his or her life ahead of them, is not in vain. We hope and pray for God's great comfort in your loss.

—Brian and Leah Foutz

Acknowledgments

Many thanks go to those friends and family who were here with us when we really needed them. We are forever grateful to those who shared our grief during a time of unbelievable pain. Thank you to those who contributed ideas for our chapter called "Helpful Hints" and those who shared their thoughts and personal feelings with us at the time of our loss. Their immediate help and strength gave us the courage to persevere.

We praise God for His insight and vision for this book as he guided Janice Havins in her assistance in editing our writings, as well as Suzanne Graham for her journalistic input. Suzanne, you have been a wonderful friend and great assistance in the writing of this book! Many thanks to both of you for all you have done!

Table of Contents

Foreword

"What is the difference between a trial and a temptation?"

Professor Helbig put this question before us, the charter group, taking the first Bible studies methods class within the new Bible Institute at Grace Fellowship United Methodist Church in Katy, Texas, that January evening.

Listening to the classmates discuss, compare, and contrast and offer personal anecdotes to qualify their reasoning techniques toward an acceptable answer to this conundrum, one particular male voice rose above the cacophony. In a silenced room, Brian Foutz spoke of the tragedy and the personal trauma it produced when his only child, a daughter, was murdered in 2004.

I don't remember every word he spoke, but I was specifically amazed by his calm demeanor as he shared details that Victoria, age eighteen, was shot because the people she rode with were convinced she had stolen a camera. Surprised that a grieving father could speak with such composure and eloquence and expound on God's blessings since that March, I struggled to concentrate as tears blinded my eyes and moistened my cheeks.

Quietly praying for Brian and his wife, Leah, asking for God's favor and protection to cover them and for His provision to sustain them, I yearned to know more about how God could take a senseless tragedy and create a courageous couple that joyously serves Him today. Something supernaturally transforming had brought this couple from misery to a powerful ministry.

After another year of classes with Brian, through the church seminary, Victoria was again on my heart. As I perused online archival newspaper records, searching for information about the murder, I made notes on a scrap of paper. Looking at her written name, I knew this story had to be told. Brian and Leah had to reveal God's mercy, grace, redemptive power, and glory through the work He had done in their lives.

Unsure about how my proposition would be received, I quietly asked Brian before our next class began if he and Leah had ever considered writing their story. With his positive reaction, I blurted out that I would like to help them write—to be an editor of sorts. Brian indicated that he and Leah had been praying for someone to assist them in this endeavor.

After a few dinners and discussions, the writing commenced, and *From Misery to Ministry: A Walk of Faith Through The Loss of a Loved One* became a story to inspire, encourage, and empower those who have suffered the loss of a child.

The Foutzes disclose their personal, private emotions and God's redemption of a comfortable marriage, which could have possibly become a national divorce statistic after such a catastrophic event. They also offer suggestions to the reader as to how to help those grieving a loved one.

I am blessed to have been able to join with them on this writing journey and be drawn even closer to my God through their project. Thank you, Leah and Brian, for sharing your experiences and the unfailing love of our Lord.

In Jesus's Name,

—Janice Havins

The Saga Begins

Brian

Even though I walk through the valley of the
shadow of death, I fear no evil, for You are with
me; Your rod and Your staff, they comfort me.

Psalm 23:4 (NASB)

My weekly Chick-fil-A breakfast with Ed the Fed, my
federal bank examiner buddy, started that mid-March
morning of 2004. Because we talked frequently on the
phone, we easily conversed about our families, jobs,
and the day-to-day struggles everyone experiences. We
spent hours laughing, especially after he said, "I'm from
the government, and I'm here to help!" I always leave
our weekly breakfasts on a great note and with a smile.

The notes and lyrics from a new song I'd written were fresh on my mind. I was about to leave for
a morning rehearsal, waiting to meet Gail, who sings
at our church. After I gave the home mailbox a quick
check, I thanked God for this beautifully serene spring
day in our neighborhood of west Houston.

Victoria, our eighteen-year-old daughter, who would be arriving from an overnight stay at a friend's house, wanted me to put a package of some of her acting papers in the mailbox. She promised she would pick them up this morning.

"*Daaaaaddy*, could you put a pack of Cheetos in the mailbox too?" she had asked the night before.

"*Pleeeeeease...pleeeeeeease...*I love you!" She used her special just-for-daddy voice, melting my heart, wrapping it around her little pinky, and squashing my ability to deny the request.

Finally making it to the church on time, I set up my keyboard and recorder and went through my latest creative music writing with Gail.

Wow! I thought. *What an incredible voice. And the song—I am just blown away! Could this day start off any better?* My emotions rose higher and higher with every note from her vocal cords. The new song was developing so smoothly; it was flowing with such ease. I could hardly wait to get it to our music group to play.

I was amazed again, unable to fathom how I was given this creative gift.

With the rehearsal over, I headed back to the house and checked the mailbox again. I'm not normally co-dependent upon the mailbox; I was just having a weird moment. I noticed that the package of acting materials and the Cheetos were still right where I had left them before I went to band practice, so I decided to take them out, and I brought them both back into the house. Victoria would be home later, I assured myself, and she could pick them up in her room.

By this time it was about 10:00 a.m. I needed to get back to work. Yes, I actually work, for myself, as an independent insurance agent. As I started working on some of my clients' cases, I felt this heavy pressure on my chest. I knew that I was not having a heart attack—I could breathe okay. I just could not seem to move. I had a heaviness in my chest, like something or someone was sitting on me. It was the strangest feeling that I had ever known. I recalled that this feeling had been coming and going for almost a week. I just now stopped to recognize it.

My wife or other friends might say, "Oh, a typical male. Never takes care of anything, especially himself. Men will complain, but they never go see the doctor!" That may be true for some, but for me—on this particular morning—that was not the case.

So here I was, sitting at my desk, and I could not seem to move. A ton of bricks was sitting on my chest. I felt totally drained. Where I had been on top of the world this morning, I now had absolutely no energy. I murmured to myself, "It's tough to get old!"

To take my mind off work, I played a computer game with no relief. I just did not want to do anything. Nothing, nada, zip!

Time seemed to slowly pass during this hour. I checked the clock on my computer: 11:15 a.m. When I heard a car door slam, I thought that it was about time Vic (my nickname for Victoria) got home. Having just turned the big eighteen four days earlier, she had been out spending the last few evenings with her friends. Anxiously awaiting this birthday, Victoria thought that when she turned eighteen, the sky would open, and she would really experience life.

I got up from my desk and went to the front door. As I faced our solid-glass door, I didn't see Victoria.

Instead, I saw two officers from the county sheriff's office walking up the sidewalk to the doorway.

My first thought was, *Great! What have you done now, Victoria?* I could not believe that they were coming to my house, and she was not even here! One of the officers asked me, "Is there a relative of Victoria home that we could talk to?"

I responded, "Yes, I'm her dad. Would you like to come inside?"

The two officers walked inside my home and told me they were detectives. They began asking me questions about Victoria. When did I see her last? Who was she with? They seemed to be looking around the house as they fired their questions at me. I insisted, "She's really not here. You can go down the hall and look in her room, if you'd like."

I had to sit. The heaviness and exhaustion were weighing me down. Those heavy bricks were still on my chest.

One of the officers looked at me rather strangely and said cautiously, "I do not know how to tell you this, but Victoria's body was found early this morning on the side of the road with a gunshot wound to the head."

Unsure of what just occurred, I said, "Excuse me?" The officer repeated that Victoria's body had been found on the side of the road in Beasley, Texas, with a gunshot wound to the head. After repeating the words back in my mind, I was utterly stunned.

In that moment, the sensation I experienced was like when I had been watching a movie. The only difference was that I suddenly realized that I was actually starring in the movie and this movie was real. Everything around me was moving very slowly, like the first time I had an accident in my car. The world around me had slowed to a crawl, but in reality, it was only a split second or two.

I guess I should have been too numb to move at this point. I should have started sobbing, with uncontrollable tears soaking my shirt. But I wasn't numb, and I wasn't crying. Staring at the officers, I prayed to myself, *Dear God, what do I do now? I really need your help and guidance.*

"Please, just give me a minute," I managed to utter.

As I gathered my thoughts, my first impulse was to call my neighbor and close friend, Bruce, who is an estate-planning attorney. I was not thinking about the fact that he is an attorney; I just needed him to know what happened and to help me sort it all out. After leaving a message on his answering machine, I thought about how I was facing a devastating situation and I needed to talk to him, but he was not home. My frustration subsided when he called me back with shock in his voice. We spoke briefly. One of the officers then pulled me back to reality.

"Mr. Foutz, we need to ask you a few more questions," the cautious officer stated.

"Could you give me just one more minute? I need to call another friend."

I called Ed the Fed, who—after hearing a quick version of what happened—said, "Okay, don't worry. I'll be right over. I'm on my way."

As I quietly thanked God for these friends in my life, Solomon's words of wisdom ran through my mind:

> A man of many companions may come to ruin, but there is a friend who sticks closer than a brother.
>
> Proverbs 18:24 (NASB)

Returning my attention back to the officers, I thought, *Man, what a job they must have. They are the messengers of bad news.*

Because I sell life insurance for a living, I have fulfilled an array of duties for my clients over the years when they have lost a loved one. These duties have included filling out death claim forms, helping them get their financial papers in order, and even assisting them in setting up a budget. On a very few occasions, I have even helped make funeral arrangements. Setting aside time to spend in prayer with them and their family members has also been a priority. But now, in this moment, I thought of these men who were bringing such horrific news to me. I felt overwhelming gratitude.

The officers began to ask me about where Victoria was yesterday and whether I knew who she had been with. I relayed to them that she had called and was getting a ride home. She had said that it would be late, so she was going to spend the night at a friend's house, and we were not to worry. I then told my story about leaving the package of acting material and a bag of Cheetos in the mailbox for her to pick up.

Ed arrived and came into the house. Stopping their questioning for the time being, the officers decided to give me a few minutes alone with Ed. Two more detectives arrived. They joined the other officers outside to have a discussion. Barry, our church worship leader, and my good friend Alan Litvak arrived almost simultaneously. We were all stunned, like deer looking at the headlights of a car right before the impact. It was surreal.

I stood there, looking at my loyal friends. Quietly to myself, I whispered, "Lord, a new saga of my life begins right now." It reminded me of John Wayne in the movie *In Harm's Way*. John Wayne portrayed an admiral of the United States Navy who was launching an invasion on a heavily armed enemy island. His staff informed him that there was a threat of eighteen enemy ships headed toward him. They asked John Wayne's character what he was going to do. The admiral calmly looked them in the eye and said, "We will launch the invasion on the island in twenty-four hours, and then in forty-eight hours, we will turn our ships back out to sea and face the new threat!"

At that moment I was facing the biggest challenge of my life. Did I have enough resources and manpower to handle this invasion?

At this point, in my stunned state, I panicked at the thought of how I was going to tell my wife. Leah was at work. I had to get in my car, go get her, and tell her. *That is not a good idea. I might not be able to keep my mind on driving*, I thought through my foggy brain. My head was spinning; I would need someone to drive me there. I had some help here. I could get someone to answer the house phone, office phone, mobile phone, and the door. I could get to Leah's office to tell her. I was confident that my plans would work, and I was ready to proceed. Suddenly, there was a wrench about to be thrown into the plan.

After the officers and detectives talked, they informed me that they wished to speak to me further and that I needed to remain at the house. The best-laid plans…I asked them to give me a brief moment. I thought of a scenario where I was standing in the middle of a room, looking to see who was in charge. And what did I see? Everyone was looking at me. Guess who's in charge?

A couple of us prayed together and asked for wisdom. I've never needed God's wisdom and grace more than I did right then to make it through this terrible storm. Ed called our pastor to get a couple of ladies together to go to Leah's office. They would have to be the ones to tell Leah, and they needed to do it pretty quickly.

The television news was now reporting, "A female teen has been found murdered in southwest Houston. Officials are withholding the name, at this time, until family members are contacted."

A queasy, unsettling feeling rushed over me. The detectives were trying to interview me again when the phone rang.

A CPA friend of mine had referred this caller who was attempting to get insurance for his wife and himself. Amazingly, I answered the call just like I normally would. After I got all pertinent information from him, I told him that I would be tied up for a few days. I promised to get back with him the first part of next week. The awaiting officers just sat there with their mouths open.

I very calmly looked at them and said, "I really didn't want to tell this client what was going on." Besides, I would need something to do when I was awake in the middle of the night. I was sure that I would have some sleepless nights.

The officers left for a while, but I knew they would return. Larry, one of Victoria's childhood friends, came by the house and shared that he had just heard about Victoria.

"Who did you hear this from?" I asked.

"I heard it on the radio as I was driving," he explained.

I prayed, *Dear Lord, please, please do not let Leah hear this on the news. She will be crushed.*

The detectives came back. They questioned, and I answered. Yet all I could think about was how I was going to tell my wife. Again, the officers left, and I saw Leah walking across the neighbor's walkway. She had Diane on her left side and Mary on her right. They were helping her walk up the sidewalk as she was incoherently crying.

"Is it true?" she asked me as streaks of tears ran down her cheeks.

"Yes, it's true." There, I'd said it.

We stood there, holding each other, weeping in agony over the loss of our only child. There was so much pain. It was almost palpable. Our hearts were intolerably heavy. Why us? Why her? Why not me, oh Lord? I reminded myself that God will never give us more than we can handle or bear. I continued to pray for His strength to walk through this, and I had no idea how to proceed on this hard and difficult road that lay before us.

The World
Stops Turning

Leah

Blessed is a man who perseveres under trial; for
once he has been approved, he will receive the
crown of life, which the Lord has promised to
those who love Him.

James 1:12 (NASB)

It was Thursday, March 18, 2004. I was working a temporary assignment at an engineering company while
RJ, the office manager, was out. The day began as
usual—the guys had me doing a lot of typing of reports
and letters. I sat in RJ's office and listened to the radio
while I typed.

I was beginning to feel frustrated with one of the
men who had (naturally) waited until the final day to
give me a large proposal to type.

After I had worked for a while on the document, I
took a short break to get some water. As I started down
the hall, I saw Pastor Jerry, along with my friends Mary

and Diane, by the conference room, where the company president was holding a meeting. My first thought was that Mary, who worked at a local engineering company, had come by because she had some type of business with the company where I was working today.

When I reached them, Jerry asked me where we could sit and talk a minute. All of a sudden, I realized this was not a social call. My first thought was that Brian had been in a wreck. It literally never entered my mind that Victoria could have been hurt. I had been praying for God to take care of her for the past two years and to bring her back to Him but spare her life.

Jerry and I sat down in the manager's office while Diane and Mary stood behind me with their hands on my shoulders. I remember being really worried that they were going to tell me that Brian was dead when Jerry said, "They found Victoria's body this morning."

I really did not comprehend it. I did not understand that it was *her* body, not Brian's. I just sat a second in shock, then asked, "Is she dead?" Jerry said that she was, and Diane and Mary began to weep. I knew then that it was true. I asked how she died, and Jerry said, "She was shot." I went totally numb. I was too shocked to move. I looked at them all, hoping I had heard incorrectly. I had not.

I began to cry and asked if Brian knew. He did. He was the one who had them come get me. I told them I needed to call my temporary agency so they could get someone to take my place.

Jerry said, "It has all been taken care of. You just need to leave."

In the meantime, Mary had gone to one of the nearby engineers' offices and informed them of what was happening. They came immediately to where I was standing in the hall, hugged me, and told me not to worry about work—I could go home with Jerry and the others.

I didn't believe what was happening; I was in a daze. Diane and Mary drove me home, while Jerry drove my car. I cried off and on until we drove into the driveway at the house.

Brian was standing there, waiting. I also saw two other friends of his, but mainly I looked at Brian to see if this could possibly be true. He held me and cried with me, and I knew then that it was.

We went into the house and sat down. I began to ask God what had happened. I had prayed against this daily for nearly two years. I just could not get my mind around it. I had truly felt God's spirit inside me for the previous year plus, giving me complete peace that Victoria would live through anything with God's protection so she could return to Him. I just did not understand.

The rest of that day was a blur of people coming in and out, the phone ringing, and lots of tears (mostly from my friends). I ended up on the back patio a lot, avoiding the crowds of people coming in and out, trying to accept Victoria's death. The only other thoughts I had were that she'd gone home and God had rescued her and taken her home to be with Him.

Our Lives Before

Leah

For this reason a man shall leave his father and his mother, and be joined to his wife; and they shall become one flesh.

Genesis 2:24 (NASB)

When a couple gets married, they anticipate many changes in their new lives together. They never think they will encounter situations that go badly and then decide to divorce. Brian and I never thought about that possibility either. Of course, we knew in the back of our minds that things would not always be perfect, but we didn't see anything major happening to us. We were in love, of course.

After only a short while, we began to see that everything was not perfect; we were two normal people who had decided to spend our lives as a couple, but we had no idea about how distant two people could become over the years. However, since we had both vowed to work through the tough times, we were doing okay.

We were thrilled when Victoria was born—a perfect baby girl! Here was a real blessing from God: He allowed us to have a child! Of course, there were the usual times when I literally didn't know what day it was; with a crying, colicky baby, sleepless nights seemed to never end. Looking back on that time, I see where a couple that was not totally committed and devoted to one another would have had challenges to overcome.

I was one of the lucky ones. I was able to stay at home with Victoria for about eighteen months. After that time, I went back to work to help make ends meet. We had a neighbor who offered to babysit Victoria while I was working. I was not very glad to go back to work, but it was nice to have "adult" conversations again!

Brian worked many, many hours as manager of an auto parts store near our home. There were long days and even longer nights with him working late. We began to not spend as much time in conversation as we once did. I felt lonely, and I'm sure he did too. Raising a baby was not the fun and games we anticipated, but we did both love our daughter very much.

When Victoria was older, things got a bit easier. She was such a happy child and full of fun and questions. I loved spending time with her in the evenings, teaching her about whatever she wanted to know. We moved to Katy during that time, and all was well again—for a while.

I really must have thought we lived in a glass house where nothing could touch us. Brian changed careers around that time, joining the insurance business. There was a huge difference working for a preset salary and working for commissions only! I admit I was not very supportive of his new career, especially because we were always behind in the bills. Finally, we had to declare bankruptcy. It was difficult for both of us, but we tried not to blame each other for this "failure."

When Victoria was five years old, she made the decision to accept Jesus Christ as her personal Savior based on her ability to understand the choice at that time. What a special day it was when she was baptized! She surely loved her Jesus! For the next five or six years, she was a little "evangelist," talking with anyone who would listen about how wonderful the Lord is! It was so cute hearing her, knowing that her friends were really listening. Several of them made the same choice that she did and committed their lives to Christ as well.

When she turned about fifteen or so, things began to change radically. Victoria was still a joy to have around (most of the time), but there were changes with her friends and attitudes that were a challenge for both Brian and me. She began to hang out at the local skating rink on Friday nights, and not all the friends she made there were churchgoing kids. Her ways of acting and talking around us became hard to take.

Things continued to get more and more difficult as she turned sixteen. Her attitude toward Brian was extremely strained, and the two of them often had arguments. I felt that I was in the middle, and not wanting to choose sides, Brian and I became less and less close during this time. Victoria began to talk back and argue with both of us, and it became obvious that she was making poor choices, both in her attitudes and her friends. This dramatic change in her was painful to watch and to endure.

Most of her new friends were experimenting with over-the-counter medications, and she joined right in.

Victoria became a different person to us. We just didn't know this angry, belligerent person anymore. When she was seventeen, it became very apparent that she was trying other drugs and alcohol. She would always deny it, but we both could pick up the signs. What does a parent do when their child is like that? Our home became a battleground and no longer a "safe haven."

One day Brian received a call from one of Victoria's friends, who said she was at his house with some other kids and that she was sick. The boy was afraid she was going to die. Brian raced over to the house, met several teenagers there, and found Victoria upstairs in the bathroom, passed out from vomiting. Brian called an ambulance, and they took her to the hospital. While he was helping the paramedics bring her out, the father of the boy who lived there came home. He was very angry that Brian was there and wanted to know what was going on. Brian told him that his son had had friends over and that they had been drinking. Victoria had a severe case of alcohol poisoning and stayed in the hospital for a couple of days, recovering. She denied that she had been drinking, even to the doctor, but we knew the truth.

Let me interject something here for you parents: *Pray for your children!* We have a paper that hangs in our home that is called "How to Pray for Your Children." It gives a list of things that a parent can pray for concerning some of the challenges that children and teenagers face in this world today. I have put that at the end of this chapter for you to read and follow. I know that God is real and that He watches over all of us, even when we are doing things that are not good. I also believe that the prayers that Brian and I offered up to Him concerning Victoria were heard and answered. Give it a try…God is faithful!

Brian and I were not doing well as husband and wife during these days. Instead of standing together, we were fighting and blaming each other for what our daughter was doing. Believe me, both of us were miserable! We talked less and less and got further and further away from the happy couple who walked down the aisle to marry years before. Things really could not stay like they were!

Victoria began to spend much time away from home with her "friends." We were worried, of course, but she did not want to change, and we were just a necessary evil when she did come home. At one point, the local constables sent her packing with a criminal trespassing warning. They had become very familiar with our house and our daughter, as they had been called to our home on several occasions due to one thing or another. When they saw how Victoria was treating us and how we tried and tried to help her change, they got fed up with her ugliness toward Brian and me. Victoria could not believe that we did not stop them from removing her from our house, but we were at the end of our rope (and our hope!).

Victoria was gone. She didn't call me for three weeks—an agonizing three weeks. When she finally did call, she said she was afraid I would not speak to her. I told her of course I would talk to her when she called—I loved her and missed her and wished she would get her life in order. She felt that she could call me anytime after that. I believe that we should offer our children a "safe haven" where they can either call or come home when they are beaten up by this world.

After about three months, she asked if she could come and talk with Brian and me. Brian was very definite that she would not be able to "weasel" her way back home, but he agreed to let her come over. When she came in, Victoria was different. Her attitude was not one of hatred or rebellion. She told us that she had spent the past several weeks living on the streets of Houston. She also admitted that it wasn't all that great and that if we would allow it, she wanted to come back home. I think the most beautiful words that came out of her mouth were, "I miss my dad, and I want the security and structure here." Praise God! She moved back in a few days later.

That happened just after Thanksgiving in 2003. The young woman who came home was so much different from the one the constables removed! She was very respectful, polite, and always had a smile on her face. When asked to help out with something, she would respond without hesitation and made the work fun. While she still spent a lot of time with some of her friends from before, we could both see that Victoria was making an effort to change. It was so refreshing to have her home again!

How to Pray for Your Children

- That they will know Christ as Savior early in life
  Psalm 63:1 and 2 Timothy 3:15

- That they will have a hatred for sin.
  Psalm 97:10

- That they will be caught when guilty.
  Psalm 119:71

- That they will be protected from the evil one in each area of their lives: spiritual, emotional, and physical.
  John 17:15

- That they will have a responsible attitude in all their interpersonal relationships.
  Daniel 6:3

- That they will respect those in authority over them.
  Romans 13:1

- That they will desire the right kind of friends and be protected from the wrong friends.
  Proverbs 1:10, 11

- That they will be kept from the wrong mate and saved for the right one.
  2 Corinthians 6:14–17

- That they, as well as those they marry, will be kept pure until marriage.
  1 Corinthians 6:18–20

- That they will learn to totally submit to God and actively resist Satan in all circumstances.
  James 4:7

- That they will be single-hearted and willing to be sold out to Jesus Christ.
  Romans 12:1, 2

- That they will be hedged in so they cannot find their way to wrong people or wrong places and that the wrong people cannot find their way to them.
  Hosea 2:6

Our Lives Before

Brian

You are from God, little children, and have overcome them; because greater is He who is in you
than he who is in the world.

1 John 4:4 (NASB)

A couple of years before Victoria's death, our lives
seemed really crazy—insanely crazy. So much so that
we felt like we were watching a really bad movie and we
were the main characters.

Victoria was rebellious and, on some days, totally
out of control. It was no longer about family; we were
not her family. Her friends were her family, and they
told her everything she needed to know and care about.
It didn't matter if they were helping her down the slip-
pery slope to the gutter—they were her friends. In fact,
everyone was her friend. Mom and Dad had become
the enemy.

There had been bouts with alcohol, once where
she almost died. She was taking over-the-counter

medicines and taking them in large doses. She was into tainted cigarettes, other party drugs, and the rap music that went with them. As a musician, I understand that rap music is just another way of expressing yourself. But when the lyrics talk of killing, doing drugs, and calling women names that I would not put into print here, it ceases to be art. It is filth and nothing more.

Victoria showed total disrespect for her mother. She yelled at Leah over little things. It was painful to see and hear. At times, she displayed pure hatred toward me, and at other times, she could almost be nice. The year was 2003, and we were no longer living in Katy, Texas. We were living in hell.

Leah and Victoria were not getting along. Mother and daughter were fighting most of the time, displaying disgust and disrespect. They would still talk together once in a while, but this seemed to be slowly fading away as well. Leah was depressed; she did not like our life or hers.

We were having disagreements and severe arguments more often. My insurance business was not doing well, and I was not selling like I had done in the past. Nothing seemed to be going right, and a good deal of my new business prospects were not buying. It was pretty bad. Our finances were, as they say, "in the toilet!" In fact, we almost lost our house at one point.

However, the main thing that was taking place in my life was that God was changing me, as well as everything that I had ever known. But I did not want to change. It was all about my pride and me. Pride was causing me to lose control and lose our money, health, and my wife and daughter.

> Pride goeth before destruction, and a haughty
> spirit before a fall. Better it is to be of a humble
> spirit with the lowly, than to divide the spoil with
> the proud.
>
> Proverbs 16:18–19 (KJV)

God had been working on me, but I wanted the change
on my own terms and not God's. Leah would tell me
on various occasions, "Brian, God will provide for all
of our needs." Yet in my stubborn, manly ways, all that
I saw was a wife who did not want to go back to work
to help out and a daughter who did not like me or care
for me. I felt like I had failed at everything that I was
supposed to be doing in life.

During 2003, Victoria was removed from our house
with a criminal trespass warning after having a non-
chaperoned party during our absence. Then she went
to live with her friends and anyone else who would let
her stay with them. Life can be really hard, as Victoria
found out over the next five months. She lived with
many friends, or new people that she just met, and even
lived on the street for a while.

Leah and I seemed to be doing a little better, but
there was still a barrier between us. About the first
week of November of 2003, Leah had been visiting
with some friends from church. Her friend Lydia spoke
a prophetic word of hope and encouragement to Leah.
She told her that in two weeks Victoria would be home.
Leah said sooner or later Victoria would be coming
home because she had been praying for this.

Lydia told her, "No, the Lord told me that she will
be home in two weeks."

Two weeks later, Victoria called Leah and said she wanted to come by the house and speak to both of us. In the past, she had wanted to come home, but she had not wanted to take ownership of her life or face the changes she must make. So I had not allowed her to come home.

When I returned home from work, Leah told me that Victoria was coming by to talk to us. I told her that we would not rush into anything and that we would not make a decision to do anything until we had prayed about it and discussed it thoroughly. I did not want to make another bad decision that would cost us our sanity and what little else that we had left.

When Victoria came in, she sat down on the chair across from us in our living room. She was very respectful, and we could actually sense and see a change in her. She began sharing a few things about what had been going on in her life and things that she had done since leaving home. There were some stories she said that she would not tell us because they were too bad and she did not want us to know.

She then said something that neither one of us was prepared for. She looked straight at me and said, "I want to come home because I miss my dad and I need my dad."

My heart melted, not because my little girl looked me in the eye and needed me, but because God gave me a supernatural peace about her coming home. No discussion was needed.

Victoria knew what she needed to do. With God's help, she was changing and needed time to make the transition into her new nature. We were still concerned that we would have violent reactions, but we soon learned that the girl who came home was a respectful, kind, courteous, and caring young lady who needed both of her parents. This was a huge difference from what we had had to deal with for the past two years.

> Therefore if anyone is in Christ, he is a new creature; the old things passed away; behold, new things have come.
>
> 1 Corinthians 5:17 (NASB)

During the next couple of months, I really struggled with my insurance business. It seemed that no matter what I did or how many insurance cases I opened, I just could not close any of them. My business prospects either decided to postpone doing business with me, went with someone else, or, in some cases, even decided to cancel the plans just as they were put in force. It was the most bizarre thing I had ever experienced in my career. Even the worst salesman can sell something, and I couldn't even do that.

In the past, we had months where we would be behind a couple months on our bills and then *wham!* I would close a couple of nice cases and get caught up on the bills so we could at least catch our breath. But this year, "It's not happening."

Leah would look at me and say, "Briny, the Lord will take care of us."

My response was, "Yeah, I know he will. So when are you going to go back to work?"

By January, we were so far behind we were about to lose our house through foreclosure. The cost was unbearable. It was almost three times our monthly house payment, which included legal fees, penalties, and our normal house note. In a moment of desperation, I sold my mother's grand piano. This money was just enough to pay the first month of the three huge payments to keep our home. Two days after I sold the piano, someone called and offered twice the amount for which I had sold it. I was still trusting what Brian could do and not trusting what the Lord could do.

It was at this time that Leah began to go back to work. Victoria was improving but still holding on to a few friends from her old nature. Leah and I were slowly beginning to work on our marriage, but not anything worth writing home about. We were only going through the motions of being husband and wife.

By February, business was starting to pick up, but not enough to make the second big installment on the house. I was going to be about $2,000 short. A good friend called me to see how I was doing and suggested lunch. Over lunch, he asked me what was going on, and I shared with him all that was happening.

He asked, "Brian, what do you really want to do in life?"

"I really want to write music for the Lord and be used by Him."

After lunch, he stopped at his bank and asked how much I needed. I was humbled, with my pride stuck in my stomach. I told him that anything he felt like he wanted to do to help out would be extremely appreciated. He asked me how I wanted the money. I told him hundreds would be fine.

While he was gone, I was both elated and embarrassed. I never would ask for money from people, because over the years, Leah and I had been able to give blessings to others. Very rarely would we ever receive a blessing.

While he was gone, I was thinking about how much he might give me. I figured that this might be about $500 at the most. Someone had actually blessed us for this amount a few years earlier. Did I say that God is good and knows everything that we need (notice I said "need," not "want")? When my friend returned, he handed me an envelope. When I opened it, my heart stopped. Inside were twenty one hundred dollar bills! Praise God!

When I came home and told Leah about it, she simply smiled and said, "See. God will provide what you need exactly when you need it." I was still consumed with the here and now and asked if she had another temporary job lined up.

As March rapidly approached, my business was slowly starting to pick up. But again, I was going to be short by $1,500. This was how much we would need to make the third and final payment to be caught up on the house note. Again, Leah would say, "God will provide," and I was still scratching my head, trying to figure out where this would come from. I later got a call from some friends at church and was told that we were about to be blessed with a love gift. Yes, it was for the exact amount that we would need—$1,500. Finally, we were caught up on the house note.

We managed to get "over the hump," as people would say. The months ahead actually looked really promising as I was making some nice insurance sales and Leah was getting some steady temp jobs. I could budget and pay our bills. We seemed to be working together toward becoming the Foutz family again.

Victoria would be turning eighteen on March 14. Our little girl was growing up, and I always looked forward to being able to spend some quality time with her.

It was around the 11th of March, and I was sitting behind my desk area in the front office of our house. Victoria came in, and for some reason, I was feeling very down. I felt like she was changing for the better in her life, her attitudes, and her friends, but it was not going quickly enough for me. She asked me what was wrong. I told her nothing, but for the first time, she pressed me on my feelings. I told her nothing again, but she, like her dad, knew when someone was not being truthful with their answer or owning up to their feelings. Victoria finally made me share my innermost thoughts. I had a huge fear that she would find herself in a situation she could not get out of and I would not be able to come to her rescue. This was something that would later become a reality.

After I told her how I felt, she did something that would later become one of the most important memories in my life. She walked around my desk area, and, from behind, she reached around and gave me a big hug. She said, "Dad, I will be okay. Don't worry. I love you." She then kissed me on my right cheek and forehead.

I spoke with Victoria on her birthday and wished her a happy one. On that Monday, she called me on my mobile phone while I was at rehearsal.

"Dad!" she said. "Where are you? I am in the driveway!"

I said, "Victoria, this is Monday night. Where do you think I am?"

"Oh, yeah. You're at rehearsal." Then, in her playful voice, she pretended to have a Middle Eastern accent and began asking me, "This is Sahib. My dog. Where is my dog? I is looking for my dog." She would then just laugh and laugh. She always had fun using different accents. We talked for a while, and then she said she would be staying with someone that night and would be home by Tuesday or Wednesday.

On Tuesday, two young men came by looking for her, but I shared that she was not home. I asked if I could tell her that they came by, but they said they would talk to her later.

On Wednesday, the 17th, Victoria called me and said that she was trying to get a ride home and would be home after a while. Sometime later, one of the two young men who had been by Tuesday came to our front door, looking for Victoria. Having just spoken to her, I asked him to wait. I called her back, using caller ID, and asked if she wanted to talk to him. She did, and I gave him the phone.

After a few minutes, he hung up and handed the phone back to me. I asked him if she needed a ride home, and if so, I could go get her. He said, "No, I can get one of my boys to go pick her up. Don't worry. We'll bring her home for you."

Later that evening, around 8:00 p.m., I was having a rehearsal with my friend "Coop." Victoria called to tell me that she was waiting for a ride but that they had not shown up, so she was going to have to call someone else. She said, "Dad, don't worry. I'll get a ride and be home later."

Around 10:30 p.m., Victoria called me again and told me that she did finally have a ride coming for her and that she thought she would be in by midnight. She said, "Dad, if it's after midnight, I'll probably stay at a friend's house and then come home in the morning."

I told her that would fine. She then said, "Dad! Could you please put my folder with my acting stuff in the mailbox for me?"

"Sure," I said.

Then, in her little girl pretend voice, she said, "Daddy, do you think you could put some Cool Ranch Doritos in the mailbox, *pleeeeaaassseee*?"

"Let me go look and see if we have any," I said. Coop was just grinning. Upon looking, I said, "No, darling, there are no Cool Ranch Doritos in there, but there are some Cheetos."

"Ooh, Cheetos. I love Cheetos. Could you put those out there with my acting papers?"

"Yes, I will. I love you," I said.

"I love you too. I'll be by the house later and pick up the stuff from the mailbox. Thanks!"

Around 12:30 a.m., Coop was leaving, and we were standing in front of the house, talking. I decided to go look in the mailbox to see if Victoria had come by. The package of acting papers and Cheetos were still there. I told Coop, "I guess she forgot to come by or she still hasn't made it out here yet. Who knows?" We both laughed it off, and he went home.

All of these events in the last few days and months seemed so strange, yet the men, the phone calls, and, yes, even the Cheetos would all become important parts to a puzzle—a puzzle that I did not buy or want to put together. But it was a puzzle that God would use to build a new man and a new woman and bring about a new journey for both Leah and me. He molded us to bring hope and encouragement to others and to serve and honor Him by bringing the message of the Way.

That Night:
Victoria's Story

Leah

Like sheep you wandered away from God, but now
you have returned to your Shepherd, the Guardian
of your souls who keeps you safe from all attacks.

1 Peter 2:25 (TLB)

Victoria called the house around 7:30 p.m. and talked
with me. She told me she was waiting for a ride but
that he hadn't shown up yet. She explained that she was
at her friend Enrique's apartment in Houston. As we
ended our conversation, I told her that I loved her and
that I was praying for her. She assured me she would see
me later and ended with the words, "I love you, Mom."

After I went to bed, Vic called the house again,
around 10:30 p.m., and talked with Brian. She told him
she had a ride but did not know if she would make it to
the house before midnight. She asked him to put some
Cheetos and a folder of some of her music and poetry

into the mailbox in case she was late. She would pick it up on the way to stay at a friend's house in Katy.

Victoria called one last time, around 11:00 p.m., and said she thought she would be home before midnight, so she would see Brian then.

Around 12:30 a.m. Thursday morning, three young men, whom she knew, picked up Victoria from a gas station in Houston in a van. They drove to Katy proper, then to the house where two of them were staying. The three got out of the van and left Victoria inside while they picked up beer and secretly hid a shotgun in the back of the van.

As the trio began to drive around, they began yelling at Victoria to confess to stealing a digital camera that belonged to the woman whose house they had just left. The three were drinking beer and smoking marijuana. Two of them started out driving the van with one in the backseat with Victoria. The one seated with Victoria reached behind the backseat and pulled out the shotgun and pointed it at her head. After some time of driving, they stopped the van. The man in the passenger seat moved into the driver's seat while the driver moved to the backseat. The third relocated to the front passenger seat. By this time, Victoria had been scared by the gun but still denied taking the camera.

She began to beg them to let her out, to let her go. They drove around for a while and then stopped the van near Beasley, Texas, on a dirt road in a field. The two oldest men got out and walked to the back of the van while the third one retrieved the shotgun. By this time, one of the other two had pushed Victoria out of the van and held her down so she could not run away. Her flip-flops were in her hands, which were crossed in front of her. Apparently he had his foot on her chest and hands, holding her to the ground.

One man took the shotgun from the back of the van and gave it to the driver, who walked over to where the third was holding her down. He pointed the shotgun at point-blank range to Victoria's face. He then yelled at the other one to lean back. The shooter pointed and shot the gun from approximately eighteen inches from Victoria's head.

Praise God her death was instantaneous!

The shooter asked the other one if she was dead, and he replied that she was. At approximately 4:00 a.m., the three got into the van, abandoned Victoria's body by the side of the road, and drove back to the house where they stayed. When they arrived at the house, one of them went up to the porch and told the woman who lived there, "It is done. That b**** won't bother us again."

At 6:30 a.m. a passerby saw Victoria's body next to the road and immediatly called the police to report their discovery.

A couple of days after the murder, the husband of the woman at the house went to the Fort Bend Sheriff's Department and brought in a digital camera that he had found inside the van. Victoria (or anyone else, for that matter) had *not* stolen the camera.

One week later, on the day of Victoria's memorial service, two of the young men were arrested and charged with first-degree murder. The third was arrested two weeks later on the same charges.

The members of the trio were arrested for the murder and were incarcerated. Two of the three men accepted plea bargains, while the shooter went to trial.

He was convicted of first-degree murder and sentenced to life in prison. The oldest, and possibly the ringleader, took a plea bargain and is now serving thirty years. The youngest of the three agreed to testify against the shooter and was sentenced to fifteen years.

Disclaimer: This chapter was developed based on what we were told by the sheriff's department detectives and loosely based upon testimony given during the trials of our daughter's murderers.

The Day After

Brian

> The LORD is my strength and my song; he has
> become my salvation. He is my God, and I will
> praise him, my father's God, and I will exalt him.
>
> Exodus 15:2 (NASB)

Friday morning, the nineteenth, started off really early, especially since I probably only slept about two or three hours. As I was waking up, looking through my daily task sheet, I remembered my comments to the detectives yesterday morning. Just as I thought, I was still up at 2:00 a.m. because I could not sleep.

Sitting at the computer, I prayed and asked God to give me strength for the day, to help me let others know what had happened to our precious daughter, and to pray for us. After praying, I began to type away, and it was as if God's hands touched mine, and the keys began to type these words …

Dear Brothers and Sisters,

We have had a terrible tragedy in the Foutz family. Our daughter, Victoria, was found dead this morning in southwest Houston—apparently killed. No other information is known at this time. Please pray for our family and extended family.

I will be e-mailing the dates and time for the funeral sometime early next week. Please place our family on your church prayer list and lift up our family. We have an awesome God, and we know that our daughter is with him now.

Thank you for your prayers and support.

In Christ,

Brian Foutz

It seemed like I cried with every letter I typed, but knowing that God was in control, I somehow felt that He would send his mighty ones to aid and comfort us in this, our hardest hour of life.

Incline Your ear to me, rescue me quickly; Be to me a rock of strength, A stronghold to save me. For You are my rock and my fortress; For Your name's sake You will lead me and guide me.

Psalm 31:2–3 (NIV)

Not really knowing how to send an e-mail to everybody at once, I just started sending them one at a time to people in my address book on the computer. I was probably there for thirty minutes, if not longer. As I completed the task of sending out the e-mails, I began to receive a few return e-mails from people in shock telling me that they would be praying for us and asking to let them know when and where the funeral for Victoria would be held.

One of my e-mails was from Linda, a friend in the insurance business.

I was unprepared for her response. It was right to the point: "What?!?!?!?!?"

I considered responding but thought about how the day was going to move pretty fast, so I took the phone with me and walked outside and prayed. I asked God for strength and courage for the day.

As I finished my prayer, the phone rang. It was Linda. When I answered the phone, she said, "Brian, oh my God. I am so sorry. What happened? Are you all right?"

She was very comforting and told me that she would place us on the prayer list at Lakewood Church in Houston, where she attended. Linda and I had worked an insurance case together a number of years earlier, since we both had offices in the same building. We would have lunch in the deli with a coworker to chat about our industry and other items. Linda was—and continues to be—a very strong Christian woman. In fact, God would use Linda later to point Leah and me in the direction of getting ordained as ministers through the Charles and Frances Hunter Ministries.

I think that it was at this point that I realized I would be okay, just knowing someone was already calling to check and see what our needs would be. This not only helped me but also encouraged me to be strong for Leah. I prayed for God's grace—His perfect grace— and His strength to help me take one day at a time. I would need His incredible strength in the days to come.

So this was the first call of the day, and then suddenly, "it" began—the beginning of another reality life movie, and it had a name: *Fast and Very Crazy*. First, Amy from the church drove up, bringing some items to our home. Helping her unload, I walked back inside, and more people started coming in, bringing drinks, paper towels, toilet paper, and large amounts of tissue boxes. I had not called anyone to bring over anything, yet they came in droves. More people began to arrive at our home. Leah was up moving around, and people were hugging her, crying with her, and attending to anything that she needed. (These were notes from my diary, March 19, 2004.)

Into action I went, moving things around to see to the comfort and ease of those who would be coming to minister and love on us. This was just one of many days that would start off this way.

I did not have a chance to get back to the waiting e-mails. I thought to myself, *What great friends we have. There are people everywhere jumping in to help us. We don't have to worry about a thing, just ride through the waves of the storm. God has provided for everything. They are here for us. They don't know what to say, but they are here and are walking this difficult road with us. We are so blessed to have a church family that is in the midst of turmoil with us. God is here—He is with us, around us, and among us!*

Then the doorbell rang. Another person arrived. We hugged, and they told me how sorry they were to hear about Victoria. I walked them into the living room, gently placed my hand behind their backs, and moved them in the direction of my wife.

"Here is Leah," I said. I turned away and walked back toward the front door to go to my front office.

After each phone call from another caring friend who asked what they could do, I told them to please come by, love on us, and minister to us. This meant so much to us, especially to Leah, because I just did not know what else to do. But I knew that I had to be in charge of or organizing something.

Friends from our life group took care of everything: setting up meals, calling people, taking Leah to the doctor, to see the pastor, and many, many other things.

Often the phone rang. I answered, talked briefly, and then I would hand it over to Leah, or I would pass the phone to whoever was near and ask them to take the phone to her. When she was through, someone would always bring the phone back to me. My mobile phone would ring, I would answer, and the same scenario would happen all over again. Praise God that someone always put the phones back on their stations; I think I would have gone nuts looking for a ringing phone!

About an hour or so after all this started, something very unusual happened. I have a second phone line in the house. Back in the days, when I had the WinFax program on my computer, the computer would answer the telephone. The call would either go to a recorded message and someone could leave a message or it made the "fax noise" and the person on the other end could send a fax to me. Anyway, this had been broken a couple of years earlier, so I changed my office number to the house number, and this telephone line was, and continued to be, a designated line for the Internet and to receive faxes. On occasion, we made an outgoing call from that line. I had not answered that telephone in probably five years. But today, for some reason, when it rang, I decided to answer the phone.

Again, there would be someone we knew calling us, asking what they could do, and I would again invite them over to love on us. With the ringing and answering of phones, passing them off to Leah, answering the door, escorting people to her, it was crazy! "Here's Leah!" I felt like I was Ed McMahon doing *The Tonight Show* for Johnny Carson.

Onward it continued, phone call after phone call, doorbell after doorbell. Yes, I delegated and had other people answering the phone and the door to help out. My thanks to Ed the Fed, Alan, Barry, Steve, Mickey, and all of the other people who helped me out. I could never get caught up long enough to sit and breathe in this flurry of activity. There were anywhere from twenty to thirty people in the house at any given time. This activity went on for what seemed an eternity. Some of the women who were there would come by and practically force-feed me to make sure that I ate something. They would say, "Eat this cookie. Eat a bite of this small little sandwich, and here is something to drink." What great friends we have! They also knew I loved ginger ale, so they made sure I was well stocked at the house, and they kept a plastic cup going for me all the time. They would even put my name on the cup, but every time I turned around, I had another new cup with my name on it. Who knows?

Everyone was taking great care of Leah. I wanted to, but my job was different. Other than bringing people to her throughout the day, I did not even talk to her. Toward the evening, God provided another blessing—one just for Leah. We had so many people coming and going—friends, neighbors, current and past church members—we could not get our minds around who came and went. I was coming out of the kitchen, and Leah had just come back inside from sitting on the back porch. As we met at the entry of the kitchen, she pointed toward the other side of the living room.

She said, "Briny, look at the couch. There are all of my girls!" As I looked across the room, sitting on the couch and floor all huddled together were most of Victoria's girlfriends who had spent much time in our home. They ate here, watched movies, went to Pizza Hut and Donut-Holes House (a local donut shop), spent the night at sleepovers with no sleep until the wee hours of the morning and then went to church on Sundays with her. Their favorite name for Leah was not Mrs. Foutz or Miss Leah—it was just "Mom." What a great moment for her and for me to see them all there together.

After an entire day of a never-ending stream of phone calls, doorbells, and people coming in and out of the house, the day felt like the busiest sale day of the year. But no one was buying anything—they were all coming to see us. My patient neighbors endured everyone parking in front of their houses in either direction and on both sides of the street and cul-de-sac. Local television stations fought for prime spots for the 5:00 p.m. news after they canvassed the area for those who were willing to share the latest gossip from the Foutz home.

Later that evening, a strange and wonderful thing happened.

Sometime after dark, I needed to go outside, take a breather, and have some peace and quiet. After feeling like I had run a marathon, I needed to go outside and take a big breath of fresh air. To just exhale, let the stress go, and just hear nothing—nothing but silence and the outdoors.

As I walked outside, I stood still a few feet from my front door. Ed the Fed, standing by the garage, began walking toward me, with his NRA baseball cap resting on his head and a can of diet soda in his hand. In the quiet of the moment, he looked at me and said, "Hey, dude. Great party!" I was stunned! He grinned, and I started laughing and laughing—you know, the uncontrollable kind of laughter. I laughed so hard I cried laughing tears.

To some, this may sound really bizarre and inappropriate, but this was just what I needed—to find something to release the emotions I was holding so deep inside of me. Moments later, while inside the kitchen, many of my male friends asked me how I was holding up. With Ed standing there across from me, I shared with them what had just happened. They looked at Ed, he grinned, and they all started laughing along with me. This event probably gave me some of the extra strength that I would need for the days, weeks, and months to come. A true friend is not afraid to make you laugh.

> Laughter is the closest thing to the grace of God.
>
> Karl Barth

Again, I am reminded of God's Word, from Ecclesiastes, to comfort us at any time:

> There is an appointed time for everything. And there is a time for every event under heaven.
>
> Ecclesiastes 3:1 (NIV)

A time to weep and a time to laugh; a time to mourn and a time to dance.

Ecclesiastes 3:4 (NIV)

Around 10:40 p.m., when everyone had left, my bride and I were finally alone to spend quiet time together. It was a beautiful, cool evening, so we sat outside on the back porch, just talking and sharing about the day. Suddenly, there was a tapping on the glass at the front door. As I peeked around the corner of the sliding-glass door, there stood patiently at the front door our favorite detective. With that, I looked at Leah and said, "Ah, 'Columbo' returns!" This was our nickname for Officer B.D. Campbell.

Officer Campbell and Texas Ranger Cook had returned again with "just a few more questions." Officer Campbell reminded us of a television show called *Columbo*, which was about a detective who never gave up on a case. It was his relentless, hard work, along with his fellow detectives and Texas Ranger Cook, which resulted in the capture of those who took our only child's life. To this day, we are forever grateful for their long hours and hard work. Praise God that they handled the case as if she had been their own child.

The Week After

Brian

You are from God, little children, and have overcome them; because greater is He who is in you than he who is in the world.

1 John 4:4 (NASB)

There is an old saying in life: "shock and awe." I do not know who came up with this line, but whoever did must have gone through shock and awe to have penned this phrase. This is exactly what Leah and I felt the first week after Victoria's passing.

Each day started off quiet in the morning. I did not sleep very much and would be up in the middle of the night. When I did sleep, it was usually due to pure exhaustion. First, I checked e-mails and sent back responses. Then the phone calls would begin some time around 8:00 a.m. and go all day long.

The continual stream of loving friends and relatives would be there off and on throughout the day. After a while, it would seem just like a blur. Someone called or came by, but then we could not remember if it was today or yesterday.

As Leah and I would start the day, we would pray that the Lord would continue to give us strength and to help us. This was important, since we knew that we could not handle this on our own.

How does anyone plan for a thing like this? There are books that have been written on how to handle things when death happens in life and what to do. I actually kept some of these for my clients. But usually no one was going to come over and share with us what to do.

Leah and I were fortunate because God had prepared me for a time such as this. Over the past years, I had been given the opportunity to help my clients go through the process of making plans for a loved one after death. There had been a few times where my clients actually asked me to help them plan everything. I was a non-family member helping them with planning the final preparations. This included setting up the meeting with the funeral home and working out details for cars, music, and other items for the service. Then I would help them go through their personal records and look for insurance policies and all of their financial information. I also wrote letters to the insurance companies, requested death certificates, got their finances in order, and then prepared a game plan on how to manage their finances.

These are some things that most people would never ask their friends to do, and yet a number of my clients placed their trust in me. I was merely an instrument that God would use to assist them and to pray for them and their families. If you have an agent or financial advisor who has been with you for a while and has done some great work for you, pick up the phone or drop them a short note in an e-mail and tell them how much you appreciated what they did for you.

As we began to talk about what to do, we decided to not have a viewing at the funeral home or a graveside service. This may be a shock for some people, or quite natural for others, but we decided to have Victoria cremated. She was such a free spirit, and we wanted to take her ashes and scatter them on a farm where she used to play with her favorite white Arabian horse named Sirocco, who belonged to a friend of ours.

Sometime around Friday or early Saturday, God did another great act of mercy and grace in our lives. He gave us a supernatural peace about Victoria's death. Yes, she was gone. We were reminded of a saying from Evangelist Jesse Duplantis concerning the passing of his mother. People would tell him that she was now in his past. He would respond by saying, "She is not in my past, but she is in my future."

> But do not forget this one thing, dear friends: With the Lord a day is like a thousand years, and a thousand years are like a day.
>
> 2 Peter 3:8 (NIV)

Thus Victoria is in heaven, riding her horse and spending time with Jesus. Then, when she comes in from playing, Mom and Dad will be there. So for us, Victoria is not in our past; she is in our future!

As Leah and I spoke about the days to come, God placed an incredible charge upon me. He wanted me to play the music for Victoria's service as a tribute to her and for him. I was extremely concerned about what to do because I wanted to be by my bride's side. When I mentioned this to Leah, she looked right at me and said, "Briny, absolutely you will play!" I told her of my concern again, and she said that my place was right there on the stage so God could use me in a mighty way for others. By me being on stage, Leah would feel comfortable knowing that the music God wanted for the service would be played. She then told me that I would be a source of strength and courage for others who would be struggling with their pain, as well as the pain of their friends and children. Man! What a cool and wonderful wife I have! I am blessed.

Leah and I began to discuss what to do for the service and what we wanted. As we talked through the late-night hours, we knew that many of Victoria's friends would be there. For many of them, this might be one of the few times that they would be in a church other than for a wedding or special Christmas or Easter service. This would be an opportunity to share God's love and redeeming power of salvation. With that, we made sure that we would have the speaking pastor give a message of salvation and an invitation to ask Jesus into their lives. We would have a time for prayer and healing at the altar for all who wanted to come and for those who wanted Jesus in their lives. As the day moved on, we were ministered to by so many people, and the love of Christ was all around us.

I later went to Kingsland Baptist Church in Katy to see Pastor Alex Kennedy and see if we could do the service there. We decided on this church because this was where Victoria grew up and many of her friends and ours still went there. The pastor's secretary came out and said she had spoken with Alex and they were there to help out.

Isn't it neat how God's grace and provision are always there and available when we need them? I then went by the funeral home and worked out some of the details for the service.

My sister Marta had called and was very saddened by Victoria's passing. She wanted to come and help out any way she could. She would be flying in on Monday and would see me then. Then my sister Claudia called. She too was stunned and shocked. She offered to help out any way that she could.

Later that evening, most of Leah's relatives began arriving. Leah's parents were there, as well as her three brothers—Mark, Scott, and Kelly—and their wives and children and several other relatives from North Texas.

I still cannot begin to thank everyone who brought supplies, drinks, and food. Did I say food? We had lots of food. With all these people coming, we did not know how to accommodate them. Our friend Diane had a list of who would be bringing food and other supplies as needed. We didn't have to worry about a thing.

Later that evening, most of the members in our music group, the Daystar Project, came over to the house to minister to us. Some time later, I finally shared with them what Leah and I had discussed earlier in the day. I told them that I was going to play for Victoria's service and wanted to know if any of them would like to come and play. After I got some really interesting looks and comments, a few of them asked me, "Brian, are you sure you want to do this? Do you think you are really up to this? You know, you don't have to do this. You might want to sit with Leah."

I looked at Leah and asked, "Do you want me to play?"

"Absolutely!"

Over the years, I've enjoyed sharing with people that my wife has trained me well. That is, when in doubt, go find a woman, and she will tell you what to do. I do like to use this line quite a bit, and I always get great comments back from women. They have told Leah later that I have given them my line, and she tells them with a smile, "Yes, I have trained Brian well, but you also need to know that he has two traits. His primary trait is that he is expressive and very easy to talk to, but his backup trait is that he is a driver!"

So I guess that got settled rather quickly.

After I asked the band if they would like to honor Victoria by playing with me for the service, everyone said that they would love to play for the service.

As the evening tapered off and everyone began to leave, there was silence. No phones, no doorbells, no one asking questions. Just silence. So Leah and I walked out the backdoor to sit on the back patio. It was a wonderful cool and dry evening, and this would become a haven for us over the next few weeks, where we would just talk, look into each other's eyes, and cry about the day, the loss, and what to do next. We were finally beginning to relax, just the two of us. It was the "*whew!*" moment. The moment when we finally just stopped and took a break from the excitement, craziness, and the continual focus and drive of the day. We could finally take a long, deep breath and exhale.

And then, there in the quiet moment, it happened again. Our dedicated detective tapped on the glass on the front door. Leah and I looked at one another and said, "Columbo returns."

The weekend was just as busy as the previous days, and so would be the next few weeks. Saturday was hectic. At the time, I felt like I was running on pure energy. I knew that God was in control because there was no way that I had the energy to sustain the drive for an all-out blitz.

As more and more friends came, I would have a couple of phone calls and visits from detectives. Leah was hoping a particular couple would come by. Our friends, Dan and Stella, had lost one of their daughters just a few years earlier. Leah knew that she would be okay when she saw Stella. We serve an awesome God! Some time later, while I was on the phone outside, a truck pulled up, and out stepped Dan and Stella. What an answer to prayer.

We hugged and cried, and then I took them inside to see Leah. Later, Leah and I would talk about who came, what was said, and just the craziness of it all. Again, when we finally found a quiet time, we rested in His presence. And then there was a knock on the glass on the front door. It was our favorite detective, B. D. Campbell, and Texas Ranger Cook. They were relentless in the pursuit of Victoria's murderers.

After our meeting, I asked them to stay but for a moment. I prayed for them and their fellow officers. My prayer was that God would supernaturally provide them with phone calls and other information that would bring those guilty to eventually be arrested and for justice to prevail. This was to give them energy and to sustain their drive to finish their work on this case.

When Sunday arrived, Leah wanted to stay home. She was exhausted and needed to rest and could not bring herself to go to church. I told her to stay home and that I would go. I did not know why, but I knew that I was supposed to go. After I arrived, many people came up to me and expressed how sorry they were to hear about Victoria. During the service, the pastor brought me up front for prayer so that the whole church could pray for Leah and me.

After the service, I did something that I thought was really crazy at first and later would see as another God moment. I went over to the youth service. Right about now you are probably saying, "Wow! What were you thinking? You just lost your only child! This would be too hard for anyone to bear!" As I entered the room, the youth pastor was talking to the youth. I walked up to the side and stood about twenty feet from him. He looked at me and said, "Brian, can I help you?" I asked him if it would be all right for me to speak to the youth. He was totally surprised. He then stopped, motioned with his hands like inviting someone into his home, and gave me the opportunity to speak to them. At this point, I had no idea what I was about to say. *Lord*, I quickly prayed, *what do you want me to say?* Then a divine intersection began to take form.

I began to share with the youth what had happened to Victoria and that there would be some people with information and others with rumors. I offered them what we knew so far: for whatever reason, some young men decided to take the life of our only daughter. I shared with them that Victoria had accepted Christ at age five and had been like a little evangelist from that time until about age sixteen. She had made some poor choices in friends, music, and other things of this world. She had been rebellious, disrespectful, and out of control, but she had begun to get her life back in order and had turned back to God for help. She was doing this when she was taken home this past Thursday.

I continued to explain that my coming there was to share with them so that they may know Jesus Christ.

"Maybe you have accepted him as your personal Savior, and in time, you have turned your back on Him. For others, you do not know who He is. Some of you do not know who I am, but I want to share something very important with you today, as a parent and father of Victoria. Each and every one of you is very special. Because all of you were made in His image, you have been given a special name and have a special purpose in this time, here and now. If you have done anything wrong for any reason, God can forgive you. His Word says that when we repent, He totally forgets whatever bad thing we have done wrong. He is not like our friends or parents who forgive us but still remember. His word says that He forgives us, wipes the slate clean, and remembers no more those things that we did wrong. Let me pray for you."

> For where two or three have gathered together in
> My name, I am there in their midst.
>
> Matthew 18:20 (NASB)

As I began to pray, one by one the youth began to walk toward me. As I continued praying, I suddenly felt little hands on my arms, on my shoulders, and on my back. When I finished praying, one by one the youth began praying for me, for Leah and our family, and for

Victoria. With tears rolling down my cheeks, I could feel two young girls pressed against my side, holding me and crying, and another teenage boy on the other side, hugging me and weeping. Then he began praying.

It seemed like everyone who was close to me prayed. Occasionally I looked and saw a sea of children and youth all around me. They were trying to touch me to comfort me. Those who could not held their hands out in the direction of where I stood. I was overwhelmed and stunned. God answered my prayer for comfort. What an awesome God we serve!

In looking back, I told Leah later that I felt like I had been in the movie *Close Encounters of the Third Kind*. At the end of the movie, the leading man, Richard Dreyfuss, is going to be taken back to another planet or galaxy on a spaceship. As he is walking toward the ship, all of these little alien people come out, and they just love him, and all these little hands are touching his arms. For a moment, I too felt like I was about to be taken to another place. I was—God's perfect peace.

Later that night, we cried in one another's arms and let the process of weeping and grieving take over in the quiet time—just Leah, our Lord, and me. (Yes, our nightly visitor came again for a visit and an update.)

On Monday morning, Leah and I got a phone call early from the Walkers. Diane was coming by to get Leah, and Steve would be by to pick me up because we were told that we could not be home today.

About thirty minutes later, some people started arriving at the house. They were not there to sit around with us for the morning; they were there to clean our home! Wow! We were just speechless.

Diane arrived, got Leah, and drove off for the morning. Leah and I would meet the pastor later that afternoon to go over the service schedule for Wednesday. Steve picked me up, and we went to the funeral home to take care of the rest of the arrangements and changes. Then Steve and I walked around the mall to pass away some of the time.

While we walked, I got a phone call from the United Kingdom. A man whom I knew only through e-mail called me. Craig, a Christian musician and writer with whom I had done some co-arranging, had called to share his shock and sympathy at our loss. His words and prayers on the phone were an immediate pick-me-up and added that extra touch of God's hand in my life. We never know whom God will send to us in our moments of need.

A friend loves at all times.

Proverbs 17:17a (NASB)

Sometime later in the day, my sister Marta arrived from the airport. It was good to see her again. She was a great source of help, and our golden retriever, Trooper, became great friends and pals with her. Trooper would sleep next to her on the couch. Trooper was Victoria's puppy—all ninety-five pounds of him—and was a friend to all of the kids in the neighborhood.

Tuesday would be like all of the other days: phone calls, more people at the door, detectives calling or coming by with the anticipation of tomorrow looming. Tomorrow would be "the service." Could it be here already? It just seemed like yesterday. Lord, I really need You more and more.

Hear my cry, O God; Give heed to my prayer. From the end of the earth I call to You when my heart is faint; lead me to the rock that is higher than I.

Psalm 61:1–2 (NASB)

The Service: A Celebration of Life

Leah

For I will turn their mourning into joy and will comfort them and give them joy for their sorrow.

Jeremiah 31:13 (NASB)

Wednesday, March 24. The day dawned just like most others. I was exhausted from the past week from people being around all the time and from a lack of sleep. Today would be a very wonderful day, I told myself.

Brian was up early, as usual, and left to go over to the church to work with the band and get things set up for later that day. We had met with Jerry, our pastor, on Monday to discuss the service. He was going to give a service about Jesus and how He could be with us in the toughest of times, even when death comes. He was going to end his message by asking people to respond and come forward for prayer. We had a team assembled to handle that part as well.

One thing that we both wanted at that service was a real "come to Jesus" message to be given. We knew that many of Victoria's friends might be there, and most of them may have never been in a church. We truly wanted to give them an opportunity to make a change in their lives by accepting Jesus as their Savior. They might never have another chance!

There would be no casket for Victoria; she had been cremated. We were going to celebrate her life, not mourn her death! It was the right thing to do for her. I knew that she was not here anymore, but I just could not abide the thought of her body being locked in a box. She was a free spirit, and it just seemed right. Brian agreed with me.

As I was getting ready to go to the church that morning, there was a knock on the door. The Texas Ranger and lead detective were there. They came to tell us that two of the men who murdered Victoria had been arrested that morning. What a relief! I was so glad that they were off the street! I thanked them and left immediately to run over to the church to tell Brian. He was also glad that they had been caught. I was so happy that we would not go through another day not knowing who had done this terrible thing.

One thing is for certain: riding in a limousine is not what it's cracked up to be. No legroom at all! I rode over to the church later that day with my mom and dad, Brian's sister Marta, and my dear friend Jackie, who had driven over from Lake Charles that morning to be with me.

Brian had given us all final instructions before he left that morning. He warned us not to talk with anyone (mainly the media). We, as family, were not there to talk to others; we were there to honor Victoria and celebrate her life. We all promised to do so.

The church was really crowded. There were people *everywhere*. The family was taken into the pastor's office for last-minute instructions. Everyone wanted to know where Brian was. They did not know that he was going to play the keyboard with the Daystar Project during the service. It was his gift to "his girl" to honor her. I was so proud of him!

When we were led out to the worship center, I was amazed that there were so many people there. I had no idea! I spotted several of Victoria's former teachers, as well as many, many others that we knew. I was humbled that so many took the time to come. I also saw quite a few of Vic's friends there, and several came over to give me a hug. I looked up at the stage and saw Brian sitting at the keyboard. He looked so calm and peaceful that I knew he would be fine; Jesus's love was all over him! There was a glow around him as he sat there, smiling at me with love. I gave him a thumbs-up and sat down.

The service was incredible! The band played, Pastor Alex spoke a few words, and then Pastor Jerry got up and began to speak. I had never heard such a tender, healing message. He not only spoke about healing the brokenhearted, but he also gave the plan of salvation and invited any who wanted to come down front for prayer. I silently prayed as the music played. When I looked up, there must have been thirty or forty young people down front waiting patiently to pray with one of the counseling team. It was so wonderful! One teenage boy stopped and hugged me as he went on to the front. He gave his life to Jesus that day, along with six or seven others. Praise God!

The Lord is close to the brokenhearted and saves those who are crushed in spirit.

Psalm 34:18 (NIV)

He heals the brokenhearted and binds up their wounds.

Psalm 147:3 (NIV)

When the service was dismissed, I was immediately surrounded by many who wanted to share their condolences with me. Many young people came up in tears, hugged me, and left. One of Victoria's best friends actually brought us a plaque with a picture of Victoria on it and a wonderful message. I probably could have stayed there all afternoon!

Eventually, however, it was time to leave. Only Marta, Jackie, and I rode back home in the limo; Mom and Daddy left from the service to go home, which was several hours away from us. When we arrived home, additional people came by the house, so it was still quite busy for us. Brian and I visited and loved on Victoria's friends at the house for a while, and then everyone was gone.

My heart was so full of God's grace during the service and the love I had for all those who loved my daughter! I prayed and thanked Him for helping the service to be just what it needed to be. It was a day I would remember always.

God's Redemption and Grace

Brian

> As God's fellow workers we urge you not to receive God's grace in vain. For He says, "In the time of My favor I heard you, and in the day of salvation I helped you." I tell you, now is the time of God's favor, now is the day of salvation.
>
> 2 Corinthians 6:1–3 (NIV)

There was a stirring in my heart, and my mind began to race into action. I did not want to think about this right now. I just wanted to sleep. Why can't you just leave me alone and let me sleep?

These were thoughts I had as the early light of the morning came crashing in through my eyelids. I wanted to tell God that I did not want to get up yet and that I did not want to be in charge of anything today. Let someone else handle a crisis for a change. Why me? Yeah, I know. You made me and equipped me for such a time as this, but can I pass on this one?

I was reminded of how Jesus asked his Father to pass on a painful thing about to happen in his life while He was praying in the garden.

> Going a little farther, he fell with his face to the ground and prayed, "My Father, if it is possible, may this cup be taken from me. Yet not as I will, but as you will."
>
> Matthew 26:39 (NIV)

As I got up and walked through the house, I headed for the kitchen and turned on the coffeepot. My sister Marta, as well as one of Leah's close friends, Jackie, would want their morning cups of coffee.

All was quiet in the house. Trooper, our golden retriever, was next to Marta on the couch, and our five cats were all sleeping peacefully throughout the house.

As I turned on the computer and waited for the incoming e-mails, I noticed the date. It was Wednesday morning, the 24th of March. I had not slept much the night before again. I spent some time with my sister Marta, and we sat up and talked until early morning. Then it was off to bed and to sleep from just pure exhaustion.

After reading the e-mails and crying over the wonderful responses and outpouring of love from others, I noticed the time. It was about 6:00 a.m. Since I had given the church a play list for the service, I thought it would be a good time for me to practice.

I headed to the back bedroom, where I had my keyboard set up, and looked at the music for the service. I placed my headphones on my head and began to pray. "Lord, I need your strength today even more than I have ever wanted or needed it. I cannot do this by myself. I need to be strong. So many people will be looking to me to lead today: the band, Leah, and others. When they see me today, they need to see Your light shine through me. Let me shine for You today as I honor my daughter in her celebration-of-life service. There will be kids today that will be hurting, lost, and looking for answers. Let them find You today and find comfort in Your love and in Your grace and sweet spirit."

Leah had requested that I play the song "As the Deer," written by Martin Nystrom. This was one of Leah's favorite songs, as well as one that Victoria liked. The song is based on Psalm 42:1.

> As the deer panteth for the water
> So my soul longeth for thee

In the past, when I played this song, I had usually played a light string sound or maybe a French horn sound on the synthesizer. I had never played this on the piano. The harder I tried to read the music and play, the worse I sounded. It was awful! Finally, I just closed my eyes and concentrated on playing for my Lord. Just for Him, not for anyone else. When I did this, I seemed to gracefully play through the song. After a couple of times through this, it became natural to me, and God was there, helping me at every turn.

As I began to run through the song again—who knows how many times I had played it as this point— something happened. It was very sad but very beautiful at the same time. As I was playing, I looked out the window toward the front yard. I had just played through the verse and chorus and began to play the verse again, and then, there it was. A vision and a memory all mixed into one. There, outside on the lawn, was my daughter—a memory of her at age eight in a black-and-white dress, dancing to the song. My heart skipped, and a pain deep down inside began to rise, and I just wept and wept as I played and watched the memory glide about in perfect stride right outside my front window. Our God is an awesome God, and He must be praised! I knew that she was in heaven with Him, dancing for Him and singing His praises!

Leah later asked me if I was okay, and I shared with her what happened. She said that she could see her dancing as well, because Victoria always loved to dance. The picture was one that was just carefree and innocent. Children are just like that, and we, as adults, sometimes need to learn to just relax and let our Father take care of us. That is His job. Our job is to follow Him and trust Him.

Later that morning, I arrived at Kingsland Baptist Church to begin unloading the car and setting up my keyboards for rehearsal. As I walked into the church, I stopped and looked at the stage. I turned to the music minister and said, "You know, I always wanted our group to come here and play for the church, but this is not the event that I was planning on."

As we were setting up for rehearsal, Leah came walking up the aisle. She said, "Briny, I wanted to come and tell you personally. The detectives had just come by. They have arrested two of the men who were responsible for killing Victoria."

All that I could say was, "Praise God!" I gave her a kiss and a hug and went back to setting up. I was still in "setup mode." My mind was thinking about getting ready and preparing for the service.

"Is everyone else here yet? Do you need anything? Do we have enough microphones? What about the soundman? Can you hear yourself in the earphone monitors?" My heart was racing, and the pounding in my chest was almost unbearable. It felt like someone took two sharp fishing hooks and stuck them on the upper side of my chest and then began to pull them outwardly, stretching my skin.

"Deep breaths. Take some long, deep breaths," I said. "You will be okay." Then the rest of the musicians arrived. We prayed, and then we rehearsed. After the rehearsal, I told everyone that they could come over to the house for lunch. I mentioned earlier that we had a great support group of men and women who came to our aid. When I got back to the house, I found out that the praise team from Holy Cross Church brought sandwiches and lunch for everyone. This was a church where I had been asked to fill in on keyboards from time to time in Sugar Land, Texas. What a great out-pouring of love and support they would become over the next year for both of us.

There were so many people at the house: Leah's parents and siblings, wives, children, and other friends. There seemed to be so much going on, and I felt like I was in a bubble. I did not want to eat, but those around me made me eat something. I felt sick to my stomach but was not sick. It was a really strange feeling.

The time had come to leave. Before I left for the church, I got in my "protect mode" again. You should know what this is, especially if you are a man. You know, we're guys! This is what we do. We serve and protect. This is our ordained job—we are given this task with the instruction manual when we become men. God gave this protective instinct to us. We seem to be born with this trait.

I quickly got everyone's attention and said, "I have to go to the church to prepare to play for the service. There is something that you need to be very aware of, and I want to share this with you now. You will be going to the church today for Victoria's service. There will be people from the newspaper, radio, and television stations. Under no circumstances are you to talk to the media or give anyone any information on our family or anything going on with the death of Victoria. This is a high-profile case and is on the radio and television. There are several detectives and a Texas Ranger working on the case, and we do not need to have anything shared outside of this home. There will be police officers and other law enforcement at the funeral, as well as people watching our home while we are gone. So please do not talk to anyone. Have I made myself clear?"

You could have heard a pin drop in the room, not to mention the looks and wide eyes looking back at me. I am sure that there may have been an easier way to communicate this, but at the time, I was all business and straight to the point. Looking back at this now, I might have thought more of the other people and their feelings, but I was thinking more about protecting my wife and our privacy. We had been through quite a bit since last Thursday, and we did not need any more surprises. I had had enough, thank you very much!

Then my friend JD tapped me on the shoulder and said, "Brian, are you ready to go now?"

I said, "Yes!" and we left for the church.

When I arrived at the church, there were about twenty people sitting there and staring toward the altar. Someone had taken a couple of large pictures of Victoria and placed them on a stand, along with some other pictures. God, she was a beautiful girl inside and out. She would have had the potential and opportunity to minister God's love to so many people had she lived.

As I was standing on the stage, Pastor Mark Anderson from Trinity Lutheran Church came on stage and gave me a great big hug. This man is about six feet five inches, with red hair, and loves helping people who are hurting. He shared with me that later, when Leah and I were ready, he would help us through grief counseling. Grief counseling was something that he did, and he wanted to bless us with this gift. After the dust settled, we took him up on his counseling offer. Leah would later ask me, "I had this large, tall man with bright-red hair come up to me, hug me, and tell me how sorry that he was to hear about Victoria. I did not know him, but he offered to help us later. Who was that?" I told her that it was Reverend Mark and that I had met him when Carolyn, our violinist, was hospitalized. I further explained that he invited us out to play for a Wednesday night service a year earlier. I added that he had offered to help us with counseling later.

She said, "Briny, I want to go see him later. He looks like a big, redheaded teddy bear! And I need a big teddy bear to hug." Victoria always had teddy bears—little ones and big ones—and like all girls, she named every one of them. In fact, at one time, just about all of the bears were named Bo. There was Bo, Big Bo, Little Bo, Other Bo, Baby Bo, and the most special one of all was Baby BeeBo. This would be the bear of choice—she slept with BeeBo, ate with BeeBo, used the bathroom and bathed with BeeBo, and BeeBo went everywhere with her. Those who are parents and have children know what I mean—*that bear went everywhere!*

After talking with Mark, I looked out into the congregation. Several other people that I knew were there. Some were from other churches, and some were clients and friends. Up on the stage were the members of the Daystar Project: Stephen, one of our guitarists; Carolyn, our violinist; Ty, our flugelhorn player; Steve E., our trumpet player; Ron on bass; and Rob on drums. Don, our other guitarist, and our percussionist, Steve Mc., were unable to attend.

It was about 2:00 p.m. and time for the band to do a warm up. I was still sick to my stomach. My chest was tighter than a drum, and I was feeling overwhelmed. The pain would not go away. As I was standing on the side of the church stage, Ty and Steve approached me. They looked at me, and Ty said, "Brian, are you sure you want to go through with this?"

I am sure the look I gave them probably came across like, "What are you thinking?"

But then, in love, Ty said, "If you don't want to do this, it will be okay, and everyone will understand."

I told him that I was fine and that we would go on as planned. He said, "Would you like for Steve and me to pray for you?"

When he said that, I felt something stir in my spirit. That was exactly what I needed right then. I looked back at him and said, "Yes, I would like that!"

He and Steve surrounded me on either side and prepared to pray for me. First one prayed, then the other. As they prayed, I melted in their strong arms. I began to weep uncontrollably, my chest rising and falling with each wave of tears. It was like waves of water rushing from the sea. Going in and going out. Some waves were heavier than others. But this had been a rush of hard waves unlike anything I had felt since first learning of Victoria's death. Even the hard waves, in the arms of my wife at home, had not compared with what was taking place right here and now! What an incredible cleansing effect God has placed in man and woman with the release of tears. It seemed to last forever.

When we finished, I felt a stirring in my spirit again. With that, I walked over to the keyboard and sat down to play. Rob and Ron were ready to warm up. I had written a song a year earlier that just the drums and bass would play along with me. It was a John Tesh type of song—very upbeat, fun, and "toe tapping," as they say.

I took a deep breath and started playing the song. It picked up in intensity, and I got an adrenaline rush unlike anything that I have ever felt in my life. It was an incredible sensation! It was a like a huge rock had been lifted off my shoulders, and I could feel myself alive! When we finished the song, I looked up. Staring at me were the members of the band. They were stunned that I had just played through this piece of music. I looked out into the congregation. By now, there were about a hundred people sitting there. They were just looking at me with their mouths open. I looked back at the band, stood up, and said, "I've prayed. I've wept. I've played. Now let's do this!"

After seeing a few more people in the congregation, and getting hugs and offers of sympathy, I returned to the stage. As I looked up, I became aware of the time, for it was here, and it was time. Leah would share with me later that family and friends had asked her on the way to the church, then later in the waiting room, "Where is Brian? Why isn't he here with you?" She told them that I had a job to do and that I was right where I was supposed to be.

About 2:45 p.m., I motioned to the band, and we began to play some instrumental songs. Many people in the congregation did not even realize that I was up on stage. They just seemed to look around to see who was there or not there. Isn't that what you do at a funeral or wedding? Look around and see who you know who is there, or wonder why you do not see someone else that should be there?

There was no casket today. The Lord had given us the right decision on what to do. Victoria had been a free spirit, and because of that, we had decided to have her cremated.

> All go to the same place; all come from dust, and to dust all return.
>
> Ecclesiastes 3:19 (NIV)

There was not a funeral being held today. There were many who thought that they were coming to a funeral.

But today, there was a change of plans. Today, there was a celebration of life.

This was a time of praise and worship. Today, all would be lifting up their voices and their instruments to the Lord of lords and King of kings. Even in a Baptist Church, there were voices singing loudly and joyfully, with hands lifted high! Praise God!

Later, Pastor Alex Kennedy would share of his time knowing Victoria and how she brought others to church, to camp, and saw others give their lives to Jesus Christ.

One of Victoria's friends, Lauren, saw her dad, David, go up on stage and share his thoughts. He told people of some of the funny things that his daughter and Victoria did. Then he finished with an incredible story of who Victoria was. He said that in life there are people who walk into a dark room and light a match so that others can see. There are those who come into the same dark room and turn on a lamp to bring light to others. But when Victoria walked into a room, the roof came off and the sun shined in! That was our daughter. And she did have the light of the Son within her!

Another friend, Shawn Walker, shared a story of being Superman and how he thought of himself as Superman—always there to save someone. But this time, he could not save Victoria. He wanted to and tried to but was not able. Only God can save you. Patti McNeal read a poem that Victoria had written. We felt that this poem was one that revealed that somehow Victoria knew that her time here on earth would be short.

"Forever You and Me"

by Victoria Carol Foutz

Until the world has fully turned
And every last tear has cried
I will be here for you
Waiting by your side.

Until the time has come
When everyone must die
I will heal your broken spirit
And free it so it may fly.

Until the day is gone
And all that's left is night
I will be brushing through your hair
Assuring it will be all right.

Floating out to sea
I will always love you
Forever, you and me.

Until the angels come for you
And God opens up His arms
I will be there to comfort you
And shelter you from harm.

Until I've gone to sleep
And I am in my grave
Even then I will be with you
My love will never fade.

Until every injustice served
And no one else will bleed

I will still love you always
Forever, you and me.
Until my heart quits beating
And my feet no longer walk
Until you no longer come to me
My heart will be unlocked.
Until there is no more happiness
And life itself is gone
I will be waiting here with you
Waiting for the dawn.
Until the day I die
Until that dreaded day
I will be right by your side
Showing you the way.
Until I leave this life
Until I leave this place
Until I am forever gone
I will wipe tears from your face.
Until the world has fully turned
And every last tear has cried
Forever, you and me
Until the day I die.

When Patti read the poem, there was not a dry eye in the place. Later, we thought that every girl and friend Victoria knew who was in the congregation that day felt the poem had been written just for them. What an incredible piece of poetry. This was not a poem for one person only but for all. Is that not how our Father in heaven provided for us with His Word? That it is to be shared, not with just one, but for all?

Pastor Jerry Edmondson then shared an important message. It was a story about a young boy who had captured some birds and was on the way home with them. A local pastor saw him and asked him what he was going to do, and the boy told him he would poke them with a stick, beat them, and then give them to his cat to torment. The pastor asked him how much he wanted for the birds. The boy told him that they weren't worth anything. They discussed this back and forth until finally the pastor offered to buy them for $10 to buy a new set of clothes.

"For some stupid birds?" the boy replied.

"Yes," the pastor said, "for the birds."

So the boy gave him the birds. As the boy stood there, the pastor took the cage and lightly set it down. One by one, he proceeded to take each bird out, gently petting them and loving them, and then let them go.

The boy said, "Mister, you set all of the birds free just for a new set of clothes?"

"Yes," he said.

"You see," Pastor Jerry said, "Satan is like that boy. He will keep us in a cage and torment us and treat us badly and take away all hope. But Jesus came along and offered to pay for us. He paid for us with His life to set us—the captives—free, to give us a new life and a chance to put on new clothes. To forgive us for what we have done in the past, and to change us for the better."

> Neither do men pour new wine into old wineskins. If they do, the skins will burst, the wine will run out and the wineskins will be ruined. No, they pour new wine into new wineskins, and both are preserved.
>
> Matthew 9:17 (NIV)

He went on to say, "As you can see, there is no casket here today. That is because Victoria is not here. She is in heaven with her heavenly Father. He is calling you today to let you know that you too can have a set of new clothes." He then gave an invitation to the altar for those who wanted prayer and for those who wanted to accept Jesus Christ as their personal Savior.

As I played from the stage, I saw many of the youth come down for prayer. It was incredible. We found out later that there were at least eight young people who accepted Jesus Christ as their personal Savior at the altar that day. Later, we learned something cool from one of the counselors up front who prayed with those who came down. He said that as he finished praying with one kid, another young man walked up to him. He was dressed very rugged and smelled of burnt tobacco or pot. That young man cried and told him, "I want a new set of clothes! Can I have a new set of clothes?" Praise God!

Again, this was not a funeral; it was a celebration of life. It was a second chance to celebrate eternal life!

> Jesus answered, "I am the way and the truth and the life. No one comes to the Father except through me."
>
> John 14:6 (NIV)

Victoria, age three

Victoria, age nine

Age seventeen, courtesy of Dan Carter Photography

Age seventeen, courtesy of Dan Carter Photography

Age seventeen, courtesy of Dan Carter Photography

What's Next?

Brian

> Be strong and courageous, do not be afraid or tremble at them, for the Lord your God is the one who goes with you He will not fail you or forsake you.

Deuteronomy 31:6 (NASB)

Wednesday was a long day. Victoria's service had been incredible. Throughout the service, I sensed God's anointing. God was truly there with us and all the way through the entire afternoon.

Just seeing so many young people come down front for prayer and noticing that eight of them accepted Jesus Christ as their personal Savior proved to me how Victoria had made a tremendous impact in people's lives. Victoria accepted Christ at age five and was like a little evangelist up until age twelve. She never met a stranger and always made people feel like they were her new best friends. And now, even at her death, God used her in a mighty way. He wants all of his children to have a relationship with Him. He does not want them to be eternally separated from Him when they die. One of the young men who accepted Jesus Christ that day passed away within the year. As a result of Victoria's death, that boy made a life-changing decision that would affect him for eternity.

Many of our friends and coworkers were there to support us, love on us, and pray for God's peace. After the service, our friends from our church provided a sit-down dinner for our family and close friends. It was a wonderful evening to just sit back and relax with one and all. Then somehow we made it home and crashed.

Once home, Leah took a nightcap pill to sleep through the night. I awoke several times and walked through the house. Walking into Victoria's room, I looked and remembered the little girl who slept there for so long. Her bears were all lined up on two of the shelves, and a third shelf contained her enormous collection of Beanie Babies. For those who might not know what these are, they are small stuffed animals with their own tags and description of what critter they represent. Kids collect them and play with them. Even adults collect them. Some collectors have hoped that these would later pay the way for their kids' college. Hope springs eternal.

Over the years, it would seem that not a time went by when a new Beanie Baby came out and we would hear Victoria say, "Mom…Dad…I gotta get one of these… they are *so* cute!" And like all good parents, when she looked at us with those big brown eyes and said, "*Pleaaasseee*," our hearts would melt, and we would surrender. Hopefully her collection will someday become new friends to other children who need a cuddly little companion.

As I continued to walk through the house, my thoughts reflected on the day. It was no longer about me anymore. I knew that I must now think about Leah and what God would have me do for her and for Him. It seemed that everything that I knew or wanted to accomplish up until this point in my life had been what I wanted to do. Now my focus had changed, and I was experiencing a type of transformation.

Continuing through the house, I suddenly found myself walking outside in the middle of the night. Restlessly, I paced up and down the sidewalk—first two or three houses on one side, then three or four on the other. I must have been out there for an hour or so, thinking about what I was to do next.

"What is tomorrow going to be like?" I asked myself. "Who will be coming over? Where do I go from here?"

I knew what to do as far preparing the final expenses, because I had been through this many times with several of my clients. The paperwork was completed. I had ordered several copies of the death certificate and had all of the bills lined up to be paid once the insurance company finalized the death claim.

But what was next? I realized that only God would provide the way. Over the years, we had always heard someone say, "God never closes a door that He does not open a window." He will always leave you a way out or an escape route.

> No temptation has seized you except what is common to man. And God is faithful; He will not let you be tempted beyond what you can bear. But when you are tempted, he will also provide a way out so that you can stand up under it.
>
> 1 Corinthians 10:13 (NIV)

At this point, I want to share something with you that is extremely important. Over the years, many people have explained to me why I should not buy life insurance on my child. I have heard this from other financial experts and people in general. Their reasoning is because children are not income producers. A parent should save enough money to pay for final expenses. In my twenty-plus years of being in the insurance business, I have seen the miracle of what life insurance provides, not only in protecting a family and business, but in providing financial peace in a time of great stress. Not only does life insurance guarantee that the mortgage on your home can be paid off, but also your credit cards, car notes, and future obligations for your children, business, and family.

In our case, the life insurance policy we had on Victoria provided us the opportunity to take a five-month sabbatical from work. This allowed us to concentrate on our grief, our emotional status, and, most importantly, our marriage. Some reports share that many couples that lose a child—especially an only child—will end their marriage in divorce. Leah and I had decided early on that divorce was not an option. We had put too many years into our marriage to just give up.

Sometime in the middle of the night, I came back to bed. Then, as the light began to seep into the skylights of our home, I was up again. We got our showers in early because we knew that people would arrive shortly.

The daily routine was back on line. The rush started around 7:45 a.m. and continued throughout the day. I felt like one of those commercials where people are walking in and out of a store, handing their card to an employee, who scans their quick purchase, and then they are gone. As before, I answered the phone, passed it off to someone else, answered the door, hugged the visitor, took them to Leah, and answered the next phone call. Today was no different from any other day since Victoria's death. I was a true gatekeeper! I have a talent of bringing order to chaos during an emergency.

The rush hour would last again until 10:00 p.m. Finally, everyone had left. The house was still. Thankfully the weather was wonderful, with a cool breeze blowing through the trees. Leah and I sat quietly. About fifteen minutes passed before we started to chat about the day. Not wanting to be interrupted, even though we were used to our favorite detective tapping on the glass of the front door, we finally decided that he was not coming and we could begin to unwind.

Friday morning arrived, and it was like all of the other days that had passed recently. I had very little sleep and began preparing for the rush of the day. An old saying I heard as a child came to my mind: "Today is like all days, except you are there!" Friends came to our side—by phone, fax, e-mail, and in person— to minister to us and to love on us. God provided so much more than we ever could have expected. We were still munching on food our friends and neighbors had brought, and we had plenty of soft drinks, tissues, and toilet paper for the next several months. Supplies were stacked everywhere.

As the evening rolled around, we spent time with friends and talked about Victoria and some of the funny things she said and did. She had some pretty funny moments in her short life. We were laughing about the time she had shown her first "sense of humor" at our expense. She was close to three years old and was learning to see things and say what they were. When we would go for a drive in the car, Leah would tap on the glass of her window and point toward the outside and ask Victoria what animal she saw in the field. Victoria would say horse, cow, dog, donkey, or whatever was in the field. Then one day, she got Leah good.

Leah asked her, "Victoria, what is that animal over there in that field?" (It was a horse.)

Victoria said, "Cow."

Leah said, "No, no, Victoria. What is that animal in the field called?"

Again, she blurted out, "Cow!"

Then Leah, after turning around in her seat, concerned and frustrated, said, "No, Victoria, it is a horse!"

With that, Victoria looked back at her mother, and with this sneaky, sly face, she grinned and claimed, "No, Momma, it's a cow!" Then she began to laugh and laugh.

Ever since that time, whenever we saw a horse, I would tell Leah, "Look! There's a cow!" We have always had a good chuckle about that hilarious moment.

> He will yet fill your mouth with laughter and your lips with shouts of joy.
>
> Job 8:21 (NIV)

The Saturday after the service started out just like all the others—people were coming and going, and there were numerous phone calls. There were many e-mails and letters with condolences, concerns, and scripture passages to give us comfort. People also sent us checks and cash to bless us in case there was anything that we needed. We had a huge box of letters, printed e-mails, and postings from an online blog about Victoria. These we would read at a later date, as they served to further remind us of the people who loved her and us.

But something was amiss! Something did not seem right. It felt weird! A strange and unusual thing happened around 3:00 that afternoon. All of a sudden, out of nowhere, I could sense something but did not know what it was. I could not get a handle on it, and it felt spooky and very, very strange. I began to look all around the room to see whatever it might be that was causing some unknown anxiety in me. As I surveyed the living room, I noticed Patti sitting there with Leah, just talking quietly. Daniel, a young man that I had been working with from the church, was petting Trooper. He had been attending our church and was making a turn in his life from his gothic clothing and attitude to one of grace and freedom in Christ. He and I occasionally met for lunch and talked about life, family, and day-to-day struggles. God had placed him in my path for a particular purpose. That special purpose was for him to be there on a day when we would need him most. Today was that day. Daniel hardly spoke, but when he did, it was very quiet and comforting. He sat there on the floor, cross-legged, looking around the room with eyes full of love as he petted Victoria's big, overgrown "puppy."

Victoria loved that dog, and he loved her. She taught him to sit and crawl on the floor to her, to roll over, and to jump up high in the air for a treat. She slept with him on the bed, on the floor, and he went with her just about any time she walked out the front door.

They were always together. This golden retriever was always happy and optimistic. When the doorbell rang or there was a knock on the door, he would go to the door, thinking it was for him, only to discover that the visitor was always for a human. But there were many times that we would go to the door and find a child or young teenager standing there. After we asked what they wanted, they would say, "Can we see Trooper?" They just wanted to see him, pet him a couple of times, tell him they loved him, and then be on their way. He was a blessed and loved dog!

As I looked around the room, that feeling was still there, and it was not going away. And then "it" hit me. Like a two-by-four across the head, it hit me hard. "It" was the quiet. It was really, really quiet. It was almost too quiet. I felt weird and nervous. I got up and walked outside. As I listened closely, it was very quiet in the neighborhood.

There were no cars anywhere in the immediate area, except for two others besides the usual neighbors' cars and ours. No cars were parked on either side of the street or in the cul-de-sac across from the house. There were not any of "those" cars around.

I came back inside. I stopped and just listened intently. There were no phones ringing—not any of the three phones, not even my mobile phone. The fax line—the one I never answered until the day after she died—was idle. I walked around inside the house and looked through the sliding backdoor. No one was in the backyard or on the back patio. I looked again; no one was in the kitchen or bedrooms or office. All was quiet on the western front of Katy, Texas.

One by one, everyone left, and then Leah and I were alone. It was creepy after facing the adrenaline rush of every day and night for this feeling to suddenly vanish. I was anxious, like I needed a shot of something, anything, to make time not slow down. But there it was—nothing. Nada. Zip. No phones ringing. No doorbells or taps on the glass. No people. Silence. Stillness. I could hear the outside noise from the neighborhood, the ceiling fan, and nothing else.

I began to cry, "My God, what is next?" I looked at Leah, and we stared at one another. We both commented on how strange we felt with no one there and nothing going on. The rest of the day was the same. There was suddenly no one but Leah, Trooper, our five cats, and me.

When Sunday morning came, I got up and left for church and let my bride stay in and sleep. She was flat worn out from the week and the stress of it all, and I needed time for fellowship, music, worship, and a message from God. More people gave me hugs and told me that they were praying for us at church. I also craved the special moments of the young kids and teens of the church that came up to me and gave me big hugs. I needed this right then. Some friends, who were like family to us, told me with their eyes everything that I needed to know. Jesus was alive in their hearts, and they were there to minister to me. They probably did not even know how much of an impact that they were making in my life. God is so good.

I returned home and spent the rest of the day with Leah. We read some more letters, e-mails, and other notes and lay in one another's arms and cried. The sobbing we did felt like a different kind of crying. It was more of a weeping, like the release of a huge stone upon our chests as we freed the tears from the depth of our hearts. I was reminded of the waves. Here they came—slowly at first, then like rolling thunder, then subsiding. Then it was calm, and the silence returned.

When this silence came, we needed to remember a couple of things. Just as God made heaven and earth and rested on the seventh day, we too needed to have a day of rest. Sometimes this rest came as a result of working six days and resting on the seventh. Sometimes this rest came as a time of day, week, or a season of rest. It was during these quiet moments that God really talked to us. It was usually when we stopped doing what we were doing and sought Him in that quiet place that He revealed to us His plans for our lives.

We discovered that if we rested in Him and abided in Him, then He would allow His rest to take place in our lives, and He could give us exactly what we needed and what we wished for. Our wish was to be strong through Him and to make it one day at a time. Little did we know that He would be preparing us for a new and incredible journey. Our journey would be from misery to ministry: a walk of faith.

If you abide in Me, and My words abide in you, ask whatever you wish, and it will be done for you.

John 15: 7 (NASB)

Restoration: The Process Begins

Brian

He restores my soul; He guides me in the paths of
righteousness For His name's sake.

Psalm 23:3 (NIV)

Another new day in our lives. We had come face-to-
face with the realities of yesterday. During this period,
Leah and I had some time to reflect on where we had
been with regard to our marriage and family life. There
had been some good years in our marriage, as well as
those "not so good" years. I am sure that all couples go
through this cycle during the seasons of their marriage.

The difference for us, however, was that we both
were willing to make a change and work hard at keep-
ing our marriage intact. After some prayer and deep
thought, we both had come to the realization that we
wanted to stay together. In order to do this, we knew
that we would have to totally rely upon God. Only
through Him would we be able to manage our lives

and time and find a way to walk through the terrible challenge of the loss of our only child.

After praying and agreeing to stay together, I felt the need to take time off to be with Leah and work on our marriage. Finding a way to rekindle the love in a relationship can sometimes be very difficult. Everything that I had been doing in the past had become habit, a routine. To break the old habits and routines required that I go through a process. I once heard someone say that the definition of insanity is the act of doing the same thing over and over and expecting different results. So where would I begin? What would I do differently? What would I say differently? Should I find a book on courting my spouse all over again?

For me, the first step was the easiest. In the past, it was all about me and what I wanted to do and what I thought. But today, it was all about Him. I had come to the Lord in the past when my relationships had failed, and I felt alone and scared. On July 15, 1981, I accepted Jesus Christ as my personal Savior. Since then, I felt that I had been successful as I had made money and lost money over the years. Then I made more money and lost more money, then made lots of money and lost even more money. It was not my lack of knowledge or mismanagement of money; it was just that we would incur expenses resulting from circumstances beyond our control.

Two different car accidents in which I was injured caused major financial setbacks. The first one took me eight months to recover; the second took me on a new journey—one that is still with me today. God is good, and in time, He moved me through a new journey and opportunity to share the message of the Way. But this time, I was really broken. As I began to understand who God is and that He is all-knowing and that nothing happens without His will and His knowledge, I found my fear of the Lord for the first time in my life. Yet I began to realize that He still loved me, even when I screwed up. He is a God of second, third, and fourth chances, with an endless supply of "repentance tokens" that are only available from our Lord and King.

> The fear of the Lord is the beginning of wisdom; all who follow his precepts have good understanding. To him belongs eternal praise.
>
> Psalm 111:10 (NIV)

So what was the easy step? It was to ask Him, in prayer, "What do I do now? Can You please show me what to do next? I do not know what to do, and only You can show me the way."

The answer came shortly, and it came in one word: time. The way to rekindle our relationship was that it would take time. There was no set period of time to go by, like three months, six months, or longer. I could not bury myself in my work and let my feelings take care of themselves. Avoidance by busyness worked to a degree, but they would always be waiting for me at the end of that period. Sooner or later I would have to face the baggage or the reality and deal with those feelings.

The solution here would be to spend time together, not just now and then at the end of the day, but to literally spend every waking moment with my bride. This would involve getting to know her again, her actions and reactions, and working on developing a positive attitude and looking for the best in life. God gave us all a very unique tool in life: the tool of choice. We have the ability to choose right and wrong and to choose life or death by accepting or rejecting Him. That choice is to fight for life and happiness or to roll over in the dirt and mud and to wallow in our own sin and go through life unhappy and afraid.

The answer became clear to me one morning. The Monday following the service, Leah and I got up, took our showers, and went to get breakfast at Randall's. We spent a little time with some of the people who normally ate there, received their sympathy, and then left. We jumped back in the car and proceeded to head home. Suddenly, a new feeling came upon me. Something quite different and unusual happened on the way back. I did not want to go back home and face the empty house and the feelings that were there, at least not just yet. So I started driving.

Leah asked me, "Briny, what is it? Did you forget something?"

"No," I said. "I just want to go for a drive."

"Okay."

I started driving toward the west end of Katy with no destination in mind and no plan—just driving. I finally got on one of the highways that headed toward some of the smaller towns to the west of Katy. The drive was quiet—no music, no talking, just the sound of the car and the noise from the road. As we came to the first little town, I slowed down and just looked around, then when I got to the light, I just kept going to the next little town. No maps and no GPS or any kind of tracking system—just driving.

Leah said, "Where are we going?" I thought on this for a moment before replying. In the past, I would have come up with a quick answer, even if I were not sure. But this time, I was silent.

Then, as if God had directed my lips, I replied, "I don't know. I am just driving."

In the past, Leah would have reacted with some kind of negative comment, but I got a surprise today. She just looked over at me with her brown eyes and said, "Okay."

I had no concept of time; I just drove. During this time, we talked of simple things, like what we were feeling and what was next. Who knew what was next? It did not matter today. In fact, we were beginning to realize that there were a whole lot of things that just did not matter anymore. Things that we once thought were really important in the past we now realized just weren't.

We began to understand that so many of the little things in life that set us off or that we did not like, we no longer cared about anymore. They were no longer important in the big picture of life. I have since shared with others that there are two constants in the universe. One is that God is God; He loves us and is in charge. Second is change. Things will always change.

When we returned to the house later, I became aware that, for the first time in years, I was relaxed. I did not want to fight or bicker with my wife. I knew that I still loved Leah and Victoria, whom I would deeply miss. Slowly the anger, distrust, and unhappiness with my wife were beginning to change. And there it was: change. Change is good and can give us a new perspective of where we are and where we can be or need to be. The simple act of driving was the beginning of something new in the life of Brian and Leah. We continued to do our "drives" on a daily basis for the next several years. Sometimes we would be gone for an hour and a half and sometimes for a couple hours. Still, on other occasions, we would be gone for up to five hours.

By being in a car with someone, we have a captive audience, and sometimes we are the ones who are captive. These "drives by divine inspiration" began a new journey for us. We would share our feelings for the day, cry about Victoria, and cry for her friends, our family, and one another. We talked about the future, what we really wanted to do, and how we could help others. We speculated about where God would lead us, and we did a bunch of laughing as well. We started to find the humorous side of life. To laugh at ourselves and surroundings, and even when things seemed to pile up against us, we would find a way to laugh.

I remember early in my insurance career that things did not seem to go right. I was beginning to feel like I was starting to see daylight in my business due to some fairly large insurance policies that I had written. Finally, I felt I had reached the success mark! Then out of nowhere, it happened. Change!

I returned to the office one busy afternoon to find that most of my recently submitted life insurance policies were going to be issued with a much higher premium or declined. This meant that the clients were not going to take the higher premium plans.

I was dejected and ready to quit when the agency manager, Dup Duplichan, called me into his office. He said, "Foutz, you are a good agent, and you have had some tough times, but hang in there, because you have what it takes." Then he said something to me that I have never forgotten. "Foutz, this would be really funny if it was not happening to you!" He smiled, and we both started laughing. To this day I share the same story and the same line with others when they are down and out. Sometimes in life we have to laugh at the situation and ourselves. It may be the next best thing to getting us out of a slump.

Our daily drives were the catalyst for the restoration of our marriage and our personal lives. The process that God used was not one I would have thought of but one that was specifically designed just for the two of us.

Over the years, Leah would tell people that she could not go do something because she was going to go drive with her Briny. This would be a highlight of the day for her on some days because we would spend that time together. It was just the three of us: Leah, me, and our Lord.

> For where two or three are gathered together in
> My name, I am there in the midst of them.
>
> Matthew 18:20 (NASB)

During one of our morning drives, Leah looked over at me and asked, "Briny, what is the name of the big, redheaded teddy bear?"

I looked at her with a smile and said, "Do you mean Mark?"

"Who?" she asked.

"Reverend Mark Anderson in Sealy," I answered.

"Yes, that's him. I think I am ready to go see the teddy bear now."

This meant she was ready to talk to him. He had offered to give us some grief counseling before Victoria's service. The time had come. She was now ready to visit Reverend Mark.

This was perfect timing—God's perfect timing. Not mine, but His. This was also really good for both of us. Mark began to see us every other week, and in order to go see him, we had to drive out to Sealy, Texas. Traveling about thirty miles west from our home, to make the ride fun and enjoyable, we would take the back roads to get there. We saw the gorgeous and stunning countryside in our drives; we saw some strange and wonderful things as well. Sometimes we would leave in time, with just a few minutes to spare before our appointment, and then go for a drive from there. At other times, we would be gone all morning for our drive and then get to the church in time for our meeting. This became one of the all-time best therapies for us. We needed to reflect on where we were and be allowed to go through a healing process for our pain and grief. When our grief became too much, we just pulled off to the side of the road and communicated our pain to each other.

As part of our walk through grief counseling, Mark introduced us to an incredible study. One of the first things he shared with us was this: When we suffer through grief or loss, one of the tendencies is to think that nobody could have possibly hurt more. We tend to think that we are the only ones who have ever hurt this badly. This is a normal reaction. He then took us on a journey of grief through the Bible.

> No temptation has overtaken you but such as is common to man; and God is faithful, who will not allow you to be tempted beyond what you are able, but with the temptation will provide the way of escape also, so that you will be able to endure it.
>
> 1 Corinthians 10:13 (NASB)

My brethren, count it all joy when you fall into various trials, knowing that the testing of your faith produces patience. But let patience have its perfect work, that you may be perfect and complete, lacking nothing. If any of you lacks wisdom, let him ask of God, who gives to all liberally and without reproach, and it will be given to him.

James 1:2–5 (NKJV)

As we read through our Bible verses, we realized that others before us had lost loved ones and were not exempted from the pain and suffering of grief.

Jacob grieved when he first heard of Joseph's supposed death. Joseph grieved as he was thrown into a pit, eventually rescued, and then sold into slavery. He lived as a slave, then a prisoner, and wondered about God's provision.

David suffered the loss of his child, even though it was a child out of wedlock and sin committed out of the lusts of his own heart. He still wept for his child. Many others before him, as well as after him, would suffer the same grief. Eventually God would grieve the loss of his only Son, Jesus Christ.

Understanding the pain and grief was important. Learning about the waves of emotions helped us walk through the obstacles that came with that suffering. However, the main part of this process was to understand that we did not have to do this alone. God was always with us. He was there from start to finish, and we could "choose" to receive His free gift and help or do it on our own.

> For God called you to do good, even if it means suffering, just as Christ suffered for you. He is your example, and you must follow in his steps.

> 1 Peter 2:21 (NLT)

As a man, I have often been blamed for not reading instructions or asking for directions. When I begin to do something that I know nothing about, it can be frustrating. I have experienced stress and anxiety, not only for myself, but also for others around me. Anger would set in, which posed more problems than solutions. When my computer would break down, for example (and I know little or nothing about a computer), I would call an expert for help. The same thing applies if the faucet in the kitchen sink breaks or the air conditioner stops cooling or the car breaks down. I call an expert—someone who works on these particular things all of the time. This is what they do for a living, what they have the passion for and the skills to do.

> Now these are the gifts Christ gave to the church: the apostles, the prophets, the evangelists, and the pastors and teachers.

> Ephesians 4:11 (NLT)

If we had remained stubborn with our choice and chose no help from anyone, then the stress and anxiety would have surely found its place. Life would have become unbearable for both of us. There is an age-old adage for this: it is like teaching a pig to sing; you'll waste your time, and it will only frustrate the pig!

God is always there for us, with us, and among us. We just need to open our eyes and hearts and let Him direct our steps.

> Let your conduct be without covetousness; be content with such things as you have. For He Himself has said, "I will never leave you nor forsake you.
>
> Hebrews 13:5 (NKJV)

As the months passed, our visits with Mark, and the Bible reading and assignments, uncovered both our current grief and past challenges that Leah and I had had over the many years of our marriage. Through these sessions, we learned that we had to take responsibility for our attitudes and shortcomings.

In looking back, there were times that I felt I could have done something different to prevent Victoria's death. I could have chosen not to have called Victoria and told her somebody had come by to see her. I could have been more of the protector I had been so well trained to be. I could have tried something different, like been nicer to some of her really bad friends. What else could I have done? I know that God is in control of all things and that all things work for good.

But even more importantly, I do know this: God loves me, He loves my wife, and He loves Victoria. He loves all of His children. He is always there when we need Him.

> But the fruit of the Spirit is love, joy, peace, patience, kindness, goodness, faithfulness, gentleness, self-control; against such things there is no law.
>
> Galatians 5:22–23 (NASB)

As our daily drives continued, I reflected on our current journey. God had really been working in our lives, and the power of forgiveness was doing great things within us. Through His redemptive power of love and grace, only He can bring restoration.

The Trial: How God Showed Up

Leah

Many seek the ruler's favor, but justice for man comes from the Lord.

Proverbs 29:26 (NASB)

In May 2005, Victoria's killer went to trial for her murder, after all the continuances and resetting of dates had been exhausted. It was a time that we had been dreading for fourteen months. Two of the men responsible for her death had accepted plea bargains, but the shooter had not.

Brian was not interested in going to the trial at all; however, since his testimony was vital to establish that the men had been looking for Victoria the day before her death, the prosecutor was adamant that he be there to testify.

On that Tuesday morning, we drove to the Fort Bend Courthouse, supported by Wanda, the crime victim advocate with whom we had been in close contact. Also, Brian and I each had an additional friend with us for moral support. I actually had two people with me, one being Victoria's best friend, April. I was apprehensive about how April might react to the trial; Victoria was her friend, and she was only nineteen years old. After I warned her that it was going to be tough to handle, April was still determined to be there and even got permission from her parents to attend with me.

When we got to the courthouse, we met in a separate room with Wanda, and then we were taken to the courtroom. As we saw the jury and the other court personnel sitting there, tensions mounted while we waited for the accused to enter.

Now, I have seen people who have had blank stares before—people who appear not to care about anything. When the shooter was escorted into the courtroom, he looked straight at me with eyes that were totally black. The iris of his eyes blended into his pupils. They were like the eyes of a fortune-teller—dreadfully mystical, mesmerizing, and somewhat eerily satanic. Totally devoid of emotions, with a vacant stare, this young man looked as if he had already mentally left this world and was just a figure of a man about to be brought to justice.

Brian was called to testify early in the day, but the rest of us waited outside the courtroom, wanting to keep him from being uncomfortable and nervous about his statements. According to Wanda, Brian did a great job.

We had all prayed before this time, but it was still a shock to be in this place. When the judge entered and we rose, I got a very strong feeling from inside telling me, "Everything will be okay. I am here."

I could only believe that this was God letting me know that we would not go through this time alone. God was with us!

The trial lasted from Tuesday until late Friday. Sitting there for days, listening to excruciating testimony conveying precise details of activities leading up to Victoria's death and the evidence brought by the detectives who were called to the witness stand, we prayed for God's divine presence and for the truth to be revealed. Each time we were taken out of the chamber, we prayed for wisdom for the jury, as well as for the prosecution team and judge. God was bringing light out of this darkness.

On Friday, the shooter took the stand. Our moral support team was in place: three women with me, as well as one or two men with Brian. The prosecutor was really looking forward to this part of the trial. Prepared to counter nearly everything the shooter said on the stand, even though the shooter adamantly insisted that this was an accidental shooting and not a murder, the prosecutor presented evidence at every turn to the contrary. His final compelling counterpoint was a note sent by the shooter to another inmate, in which he told the inmate to call up "his victim's ghost." In the shooter's handwriting, the note sealed the deal; the shooter had been trapped in his web of lies. There was nothing more to say. The defense attorney had nothing to add to the defense either.

When we took a break for lunch, the prosecution team came into the room where we sat and asked me to take the stand before the jury went out for deliberations. I had no desire to do so, but they explained that the jury needed to see who I was and what I had to say. I agreed and reentered the courtroom apprehensively but ready for whatever the attorneys asked. The prosecutor was careful to ask me what he thought the jury might want to know about my relationship with Victoria. I was able to tell the jury about the closeness that we shared, even when Vic was going through the worst times. I also told them that we knew where she was and that we would see her again in heaven.

Then time came for the closing arguments. The defense attorney had little to say. The prosecutor held up the shotgun used in the murder, pointed it in the direction of the jury box, and with a commanding voice, captured the ears of everyone in the courtroom. His intense and chilling reenactment of the actual shooting came to an abrupt halt when he yelled, "Bang!" This left a disturbing stain on the minds of the jury.

When the jury went out to deliberate, we sat in the courtroom, waiting. We did not have to wait very long. In less than twenty minutes, the jury came back in with a verdict: guilty.

Wow! Even the prosecutor was moved nearly to tears and so overcome that the judge almost called a recess for his sake. After he rallied, the judge charged the jury members with their duty to set the sentence. To the jury chamber, they marched.

We sat for a while and then decided to run across the street and get something to eat. We thought we had plenty of time; however, just as we got the meals, we were called back to court.

The shooter was given life in prison! An enormous sigh of relief could be heard among members of the audience. As I watched the shooter being led out of the courtroom, I was relieved that it was finally over—at least for us.

How and when did God show up? During our breaks, we had the opportunity to visit with several of the court personnel. What we found out was incredible! For instance, the lead court reporter had lost a daughter to a drunk driver, and the judge himself had lost a son a few years before in a single-car accident. Those instances alone would be amazing; however, there were more.

A couple of months after the trial, Brian got a call from a friend of ours who lives in New Territory, Sugar Land. She had spoken with a friend who had a story to share with us. The friend had served as a jury member at the trial. The jury had been composed of twelve random Fort Bend residents. *Every one* of them was a born-again believer in Christ! Each time they had entered the deliberation room, they always opened with prayer and dismissed with prayer. They had a picture of Victoria that sat on the conference table in order to humanize her for them. The only question that they asked the judge to clarify was to find out which sentence was worse: ninety-nine years in jail or life. This former juror told our friend that it was very evident that God was in that room with them and that He was in charge of the trial. Later we found out that several of the court personnel were also believers. God is amazing!

The trial was tough for us to handle, but we all felt God's arms around us during that week. His justice was done, and He had won the case against evil!

> You intended to harm me, but God intended it for good to accomplish what is now being done, the saving of many lives.
>
> Genesis 50:20 (NIV)

For my part, I do not hold malice toward those young men who killed my daughter. I have learned from reading the Bible that we do not wage war against mankind who does evil but against the forces of darkness, evil, and wrongdoing. I can forgive them because I know how hard it is to stand against evil, and because God asks us to forgive. That is not for their sakes but for ours. I can rest easier knowing that God is still in control, even when evil is present.

As we left the courtroom that night, each of the jurors came out to see us. As they passed by, we were hugged many times. We also noted that each person who was on the jury was in tears—tears of sorrow for our loss. That was a special time for those of us who lived with the loss of our daughter and friend. Thank you, God!

> "For I know the plans I have for you," declares the LORD, "plans to prosper you and not to harm you, plans to give you hope and a future."
>
> Jeremiah 29:11 (NIV)

Preparing the Way/
The Wilderness Trail

Brian

Sight is a function of the eyes; vision is a function
of the heart. Vision generates hope in the midst of
despair and provides endurance in tribulation.

Dr. Myles Munroe
The Principles of Power and Vision

What a great way to look at life!

I remember being told when I was younger that if
I wanted to become successful, I needed to find something that I liked to do and go do it. Others would later
tell me that what I wanted to do was not right because
everybody else was doing it and that I needed to find
something different to do. Various people told me that
I needed to find a new thing or new business. What
I have found out is this: All things come from God.
All things are given by Him, and we have been given a
purpose to be used by Him. We need to ask Him for a
vision. He will give us the vision, a promise, and a plan

to make this come to pass. All we need to do is to be open, willing, and obedient to be used by Him.

God has taken Leah and me on an incredible journey. I was thinking about Joseph the other day and how cool it was that he became the second most powerful man in Egypt, next to Pharaoh. First, Joseph was a Hebrew, not an Egyptian. Second, he did not have any wealth or power or an army. Third, he did not worship the Egyptian gods or live by their customs. As the youth of today would say, "Yo, dude! He's, like, the bomb of the Nile!" But the story was not about who he had become but what he had to go through to get there.

In the twenty years that I have spent in the insurance business and the thirteen years prior in retail, I have had a chance to read, listen to, and watch tapes of some of the top-selling sales professionals in the USA. I have even been fortunate enough to meet a few of them face-to-face. A great deal of the time, they will tell their audiences that in order to get to the top of the mountain of success, one must travel through the swamps and the desert. We have to go through the junkyards, mean streets, and jungles to get to the cool castle on the top of the hill. We will never get something for nothing, and to get to the top, and to finish the race, we will have to overcome many obstacles along the way.

Joseph was treated badly by his own family when he shared the vision that God had given him. We can imagine the scene at the dinner table when Joseph told his brothers his new, great news. "Hey! God showed me a vision. All of you will be bowing down to me and serving me!" Later, after his loving brothers threw him into the pit, he was probably telling himself, "Man! What I was thinking?"

Sometimes, when God gives us a vision, it may not be the right time to share it with the rest of the world. But when He does give us a vision, it will be something just for us, and it may prove yet to come.

This next part of the journey for Leah and me would be one of preparing for the future. God was beginning to show us what he had in store for us. We would have never thought to prepare for this kind of future.

As time went by, we would receive a phone call here and there asking if we had an interest in speaking to someone who had just recently lost a child. Leah and I would go and visit the hurting family, hear their story, pray with them, and then, when the time was right, we would share our story.

We have found over these past six years that when we first started to share our story, it was hard for us. But then God would supernaturally give us the strength to get through the story with love and a peace that goes beyond all understanding.

Hearing others share their stories would bring back our pain, but the pain we felt seemed to be more for them than for us. To see their hurt, anger, and the feelings of hopelessness displayed on their faces, in their body language, and in their shuttering voices set us back at times. But knowing that we have a loving Father, who is right there with us and with them, always gave us the inspiration to continue. We had to be strong for them as we shared the knowledge that God still loved them and cared for them and hurt just as badly as they did for their loss.

Who gets the blessing? Since Victoria's passing, several people have asked us how we are doing, how we have been, or if we are okay. Thankfully, we are able to tell them that we are blessed! God has given us an enormous peace about Victoria's death, and He has opened the doors for a great ministry for us. Sometimes, when we have been at the grocery store, we have seen people who know us do a U-turn and deliberately go down another aisle. We have come to understand that they either did not see us or they were afraid to ask us anything because they just didn't know what to say. Some were very uncomfortable attempting to talk to us, fearing they were going to hear a really sad sob story. After these types of incidents, I asked myself, "Who gets the blessing? Who misses the blessing?"

As Leah will confirm, I am not a shy person. Without pause, I would go right down the aisle and tell the person how glad I was to see them. I was being very genuine, because I care about people and how they are doing. Then, when they would ask how we were doing, I would tell them, "Leah and I are doing great! We are so blessed!" Often then I shared with them all that we were doing in our ministry, with our music ministry through the Daystar Project, and the wonderful opportunities God had opened up for us to help other people.

One time, while I was in an office supply store, I met a friend from a previous church. He was stunned to see me out and about. He quietly asked how we were coping with our loss. I shared with him how God gave us a supernatural peace within forty-eight hours of Victoria's death and that we knew where she was. She was in heaven with our Lord, Jesus Christ. I explained further that she was not in our past but in our future. God had given us an attitude of gratitude to be able to help others handle grief and to share the message of the Way. While we were talking, one of the store clerks kept inching closer and closer, pretending to straighten the shelves. After a short time, I saw his shoulders moving up and down, only to see that he was crying and unable to move.

God uses our story to bless others. We want people to see Jesus in our faces, in our actions, in our speech, and, most importantly, in the prayers that we lift up to Him. Afterward, this same friend confirmed what we had recently experienced with other people. He stated, "You know, I was not going to come up to you. I just didn't know what to say, and honestly, I was afraid to get caught up in a long, sad story. But I have to tell you that I am blessed! I feel like I have been given a burst of energy. What a blessing!"

On another occasion, good friends of ours, Glen and Melinda, came by the house and wanted to minister to us. Glen began to share with me concerns he had about taking a mission trip and was not sure if he really wanted to go. He was not sure if he could really make a difference and questioned whether spending the time would be worth it. As we talked about his future trip, I shared with him that God is in control and that we do not always know why we are doing what we are doing. But wherever we go, He is there. He will equip us for anything and everything. We end up at a certain place because we are obedient and willing to help and to be used by Him. Sometimes we think that we are there to help those who are in need and to bless them when, in fact, we are the ones who will be blessed. Praise God!

Again, I shared with Glen the peace God gave to Leah and me and how He was taking us on a new journey through a period of restoration and preparation for the future. "It is not about me," I explained, "but it is all about Him."

When we got through sharing, he looked at me and said, "Brian, I got to tell you. I came by tonight to minister to you and to see what I could do to help. But I am the one who got ministered to tonight, and I got a blessing that I did not expect."

> From the fullness of his grace we have all received
> one blessing after another.
>
> John 1:16 (NASB)

This past year, I had gone to one of the local video stores to get a couple of movies for the night. As I walked outside, I got into my truck, put the key in the ignition, and turned it on. *Click, click.* Oh no! Please start! *Click, click,* and then a slow *click*...no battery. No juice. I was going nowhere!

I tried to call Leah on my mobile phone, but she was not to be found. I tried a couple of other people, and nothing was happening on those numbers either. Rats! After I walked to a local oil change store and discovered that they could not help, I tried another shop a block down. Returning to the truck, I sat in the front seat for a moment and asked God for help. "I know there is something here, God. You are going to show me something, but I do not know what." I said to myself, "Self, be patient, relax, take a deep breath. Breathe in... breathe out...okay...let's go, God. We will see who can help."

I went back inside the video store and asked the manager if he had any jumper cables. He said no, and he even tried to call a friend who might have some.

His friend did not have any either because his wife had taken the other vehicle with the cables. This was odd, he muttered, because she usually did not take that car.

After I walked back outside, I thought about how far I was from the house and figured it would be a pretty warm mile-long trip on the hot pavement back to our home. Just then, I heard someone yell, "Sir? Sir?" I turned around, and a woman was walking out of the store. "Do you need a jump for your car? I have some cables in our van."

"Thank you very much," I replied. She and her husband pulled their van around to my truck. We tried several times to get the truck started but to no avail. I thanked them for their time and proceeded to lock up the truck and leave. Finally, I called the local dealership and asked them to send a wrecker over to pick up the truck and fix whatever it needed. Remember what I said earlier: if you are not sure of what you are doing, call an expert. So I did.

As I started to walk out of the parking lot, the same woman approached me again. She said, "Do you need a ride? We could take you home, if you would like." I quickly hopped in the van, and we headed for my house. While in the van, the woman began to talk to me about how her and her husband's life had been hard with some financial struggles. She shared with me that she had just finished a two-year struggle caring for one of her dying children. The child had recently died, and they had one other small child at home. This woman was depressed and not sure if God really cared. She just was uncertain about the future and what to do next. It had been very painful, not only for her and her husband, but especially for their other child. By the time they had pulled into my driveway, she had just finished telling her story.

At this point, most people I know would have said, "I am so sorry to hear about your daughter. Thank you for sharing with me. I will pray for you. Again, thank you for the ride home." Then they would have gotten out of the van and walked into the house. Thinking that this was a sad story, they would have probably shared with their spouse. In fact, there was a point in my life that I would have done the very same thing.

But not today! She was seated in the backseat, and I had been given the opportunity to sit up front. As I turned in my chair, I began to share with her that God loves her and He really understands what she is going through. "He is here right now, in this van, at this very moment." I told her that I wanted to bless her with a CD titled *He Is Here* from our music group. Continuing, I explained that God understands all she was going through and wanted to help her walk through this pain. He had a great journey ahead for her. I then asked to see a picture of the child that they had just lost. She cried and pulled out a wonderful picture of the child that was now with our Lord. I shared with them about our story. How, after losing our only child, God gave us a supernatural peace about her passing and her murder. I testified that He is in the midst of everything we do and that He can heal any broken heart and restore all that had been taken. I shared with her that Christ could heal their broken hearts and that His abilities go beyond all understanding.

Inviting them both to come into the house, I showed them our girl. When they walked into our home, they saw the two large pictures of Victoria with her great smile. Her captivating smile was a gift that God had given her. I told them, "When she walked into a room, the roof came off, and the Son shined in." They were stunned and stood there in silence. I then asked if I could pray for them.

A wonderful gift that God had given me since Victoria's death was an incredible voice for prayer. Even my wife has shared that when I pray, my voice changes, and I do not sound like myself. I sometimes do not even feel like they are my words. This happened while I was praying for this couple. They were weeping, but when the prayer was over, they were smiling and hugging. They thanked me all the way out to the van and thanked me again as they drove off.

I did not know who these people were. I had never seen them before, and I have never seen them since. This is what I like to call a "divine intersection." This is an intersection in the highway of life when God brings us across someone's path. This intersection may be for us to give confirmation to someone, to lift them up, to edify or encourage them, to pray for them, or to give them a blessing. Sometimes this may be for our benefit and for us to be blessed.

As I mentioned earlier, "Who gets the blessing?" Does it really matter? Besides, it is all for Him and for His glory.

Wise Counsel

Leah

> Whoever is wise, let him heed these things and
> consider the great love of the Lord.
>
> Psalm 107:43 (NIV)

I know what you may be thinking: "I don't need to see
a counselor! They only mess with your head and don't
really help at all." However, don't be so quick to pass
this up. Counseling can be a very important way of
helping us to heal.

Brian and I met with a counselor for several months
after Victoria's death. Pastor Mark helped us to look
at our grief in new ways and encouraged us to work
out some huge challenges that we had in our marriage.
One of the saddest things I found out was that another
couple we knew had divorced soon after their son
was killed. I know that they did not choose to get any
counseling after his death. A counselor can help you to
recognize different stages of grief, how to get through
them, and possibly help you to heal.

While some people can face their grief better than others, I believe that having someone you can talk with about the deepest feelings of pain is a good thing. Sometimes it helps to have a person with no direct attachments to your situation, like a counselor, to talk to. They will not judge you or your feelings and may be able to help you deal with the situation in a more constructive way.

One of the first emotions that I felt was shock. I could not believe that Victoria was dead. The next thing I remember feeling was the unimaginable sorrow that her young life had ended so soon and so need-lessly. Through Pastor Mark's counseling, I was able to understand that this was a natural reaction to a terrible event. It made me feel that I was not losing my mind! I learned to stop and pray for comfort from the Lord, and eventually I would feel better.

Readjustment gradually comes, but the scar is still there. There will come times when waves of grief will hit and may be very emotional. This is normal.

It is very important to remember that grief happens. We may go along for days and days without feeling that emptiness; then, all of a sudden, a wave of pain washes over us without warning. Everything seems to stop, and we are unable to function for a while. This is normal. There is nothing to be ashamed of, and no explanation is needed for anyone. Others will try to understand as well as they can. What is important is that we do our best not to fight the pain. We have pain for a reason, and fighting it only makes it worse.

In the second year after Victoria's death, Brian and I went to a Christian counselor named Carolyn Rowe, who was with a Christian counseling center near our home. Having Christian counselors was very important for both Brian and me. Through the guidance of Pastor Mark and Carolyn, we learned a lot about how God cares for us, even in the worst of times. They were very compassionate and took the time to listen. These sessions were not about what we should be doing; they were about helping us to work through the grief process and reorder our lives based on the "new normal." That means that while life is never the same as before, it can and will be happy and good again.

I recommend that anyone who suffers the loss of a child seek counseling. We have come to know several other families who have experienced the loss of a child. The ones who did seek some counseling, even for a short time, seemed to have collected more "tools" to use through the grieving process. The couples who did not choose counseling seemed to have a tougher time accepting the "new normal" place where their lives existed. Healing seemed to take longer.

I know it's difficult—I have been there! However, it is so helpful to go down that path with someone who can help guide you and be there when you need to cry on a shoulder. Having someone who is totally objective to talk with is very helpful in working out where you are and where you are going.

> The Lord is near to the brokenhearted, and saves those who are crushed in spirit.
>
> Psalm 34:18 (NASB)

Riding the Wave

Brian

But he was pierced for our transgressions, he was crushed for our iniquities; the punishment that brought us peace was upon him, and by his wounds we are healed.

Isaiah 53:5 (NIV)

Have you ever been to the beach, sat upon the sand, and listened to the waves of the ocean? If you close your eyes and just listen, you can hear the sea wash ashore. If you listen hard enough, it sounds like the wave is far, far away; then, as it approaches the land, the sound picks up, and the intensity of the wave seems to get bigger and bigger until it washes ashore. Then the sound subsides, and it becomes quiet again.

Our emotions can sometimes be just like these waves. After a trauma or loss, we may find ourselves feeling like those waves. Emotions seem to come out of nowhere, and they are suddenly upon us. We can try to block the wave or let go and let it take its natural flow.

I have heard some people share that it is important that when these waves come to let them take their natural course and experience the waves. This is God's way of cleansing, restoring, and helping us to get better and to heal. We have to learn to let go so that we can grow. The counselors that Leah and I talked with shared that if we do not let the release come, then we suppress that which needs to get out, and we will find our hearts getting a little harder each time. Sooner or later those hidden feelings will begin to cause other challenges in our lives and will later surface with or without our knowledge or permission.

I have learned some interesting lessons about waves. Besides the heavy waves that came in the privacy of my home and quiet place, huge ones crashed hard upon my heart when I was alone. My mind wandered, and the evil one lurked about me, speaking doubt. There were waves that came at different times when I least expected them, and I found myself trying hard to cope.

There were times that Leah and I would weep in each other's arms and cry uncontrollably until our chests and stomachs ached with throbbing pain. Then, at other times, the waves came, but they would seem like little ripples washing ashore on the beach.

One of my first waves came while in the grocery store after Vic died. As I was walking down the grocery store aisle, I was thinking, *Tonight will be snack food time*! My mind was fixed on little smoky sausages, corn chips (the big scoop kind), onion dip, and cheese for queso dip. As I prepared to turn the corner to go to the back of the store, hanging on the end of the aisle were packages of pepperoni slices. Overtaken with emotion, I just stopped, stood there, and started crying. I then tried to compose myself and clear my eyes of the waves of water pouring forth.

Victoria used to take pepperoni slices and strategically place them on a plate, starting from the center of the plate, putting them in a circle until the plate was full. Then she would take some grated sharp cheddar cheese and sprinkle this on top of the meat. After she placed them in the microwave and nuked them, she would say, "Voilà!" She called them "pep rolls." Being one of her all time favorite snacks, she made them for April and all of the other girls who would come by the house to visit.

Sometime right after Victoria's passing, I walked through a local store, looking for new sheets for our bed. Suddenly, my eyes caught someone walking past at the end of another aisle. As I peeked around the corner, I saw someone who looked just liked Victoria! *Oh my God*, I thought to myself. As this girl quickly moved to the next aisle, my heart practically leapt out of my chest. With a pounding heart, anxiety was building up, and I was beginning to feel a heaviness around my heart. I followed her. I only got a glimpse from the back, and then she moved to the next aisle. *God, what am I doing?*

Then, as this young teenager walked around to the next aisle, I followed her from the other end around to the next aisle. My heart sank. She looked like Victoria from the back—the height, blonde hair, and the way she walked. Reality came crashing down. As she turned to her friend, I knew that this was not Victoria. I thought to myself, *Lord, am I going crazy? Is this going to continue to happen again every time I go out? Lord, please help me. I miss her so much, and I cannot do this on my own. I really need your help here!* As I walked away, my emotions subsided, and God filled me with his love, as He reminded me from His Word that He still loved me and that He would never leave me.

Okay, I thought. *I am outta here!* So I walked the cart back to the front of the store and headed for my car to compose myself and to drive to the next stop. I hoped that a change of scenery and a short drive would clear my head and take my thoughts off Victoria. I reasoned that if I could keep focused on some other things, I would be okay until I got home. Then it wouldn't matter if I lost it at home. I would be home and could deal with my emotions there.

There is an old saying that things happen in sets of threes. On this particular day, I experienced just such a set of three. It took me about fifteen minutes to get to the next store. As I looked again for those sheets for our bedroom, I noticed a leopard-skin pattern of sheets. Oh no. Here it came—the whirling emotional wave! Victoria loved this pattern. *This is so not fair, Lord!* I was not looking for this, and yet there it was: another memory of our daughter, things that she liked, and another huge wave of emotion!

The last thing I wanted was to feel like this, especially right there and then. Suddenly, without warning and not thinking, I blurted out, "To hell with this!" I walked out of the sheets section and went to the other side of the store. I thought, *Whew, what just happened? What was I thinking?*

The picture frame aisle was my next stop to find frames for pictures to put up at the house since it was being repainted and new floors were being installed. (Yeah, I know. Right about now, you may be saying to yourself, "What was he thinking?" Duh! Sometimes I am just a little slower than others.) As I walked down the aisle, I found some really cool frames and thought they would spruce up the place. Then there it was: a huge frame—twice the size of a poster—with all sorts of little squares and round slots to put photos in. I looked at the manufacturer's pictures inside this frame—pictures of a man and woman, a marriage, a baby, more children, and pictures at different stages of their lives through high school graduation. My eyes scanned the final photo—the bridal portrait of the daughter. The intense storm of emotions ran wild in my head, chest, and heart. The heaviness was unbearable.

Again, without warning, I blurted out, "To hell with this!" I walked out of the frame section and walked toward the front of the store, all the time talking to myself under my breath. There were probably people looking at me like I was some kind of nut fresh out of the crazy clinic. They must have been looking around for the guys in the white clothes to come and pick me up!

"This looks safe," I mumbled to myself as I entered the hairbrush section. I searched the racks for just the right hairbrush, one that both Leah and I could use. We often shared hairbrushes in our family. Victoria would always borrow mine. It did not matter how many brushes I bought for her or how many she had—she would always borrow mine. She liked using my hairbrush. I would ask her, "Vic, why can't you use your own hairbrush?" and she would say, "Dad! I like yours!" She never kept my hairbrush; she would just use it. With the drama involved in having a teenage daughter, I often had to make decisions about which battles I wanted to fight. This was one battle that I would have never won anyway, especially when she flashed me those big brown eyes and said, "Daaadddy, please?"

As I looked and looked for the right brush, testing the bristles and texture, I noticed two women standing in the aisle, watching me. Again, I must have been mumbling my thoughts out loud. *This will pass,* I thought. Finally, I found something on the bottom shelf. What a cool-looking three-piece set. It had a large brush, a small brush, and a really nice little hand comb. In my excitement with my great find, I thought, *My girls will love this set, because dad always brings back cool stuff.*

"Yes, Victoria…*what?*"

I threw the three-piece brush set back to the bottom of the shelf, and those four nasty words rang out, "To hell with this!"

As I left the aisle to storm out of the store, I noticed the two women with their mouths agape looking stunned with eyes as big as silver dollars! I imagined later that they must have thought that I was a real piece of work. When I got in the car, I broke down and wept. I cried until my chest, heart, and stomach ached.

As I drove home, I spoke out loud to my Lord and asked for forgiveness for the way that I spoke and acted in the store. I finished my prayer time with Him and was reminded of something that Leah would say to me. "Briny, feelings are not right or wrong. They are just feelings." She had shared this line with many people over the years. And at this moment, it was a comfort to me.

Leah and I found that sometimes we could control the waves; however, we discovered it was best to allow them to come and go. We never knew how big or how small they would be. But with the passing of each wave, our bodies cleansed themselves and helped to restore that which was lost.

Our God is a mighty God, and He must be praised. Our sins are washed by His blood.

> Though your sins be as scarlet, they shall be as white as snow.
>
> Isaiah 1:18 (NASB)

I am reminded of the words from the old hymn:

> Jesus paid it all
>
> All to him I owe.
>
> Sin had left a crimson stain
>
> He washed it white as snow.

As you can tell, "waves happen." When they come, just let them happen and ride them out. Realize that the waves will eventually taper off and your emotions, like the waves, will wash ashore.

Our Ministry Begins

Leah

> Blessed be the God and Father of our Lord Jesus Christ, the Father of mercies and God of all comfort, who comforts us in all our affliction so that we will be able to comfort those who are in any affliction with the comfort with which we ourselves are comforted by God.
>
> 2 Corinthians 1:3–4 (NASB)

I will never forget the first phone call we received. It was from a good friend, Melinda, who was very involved with The Compassionate Friends in Katy (The Compassionate Friends have groups all over the country). Melinda called us to see if we would be willing to go see a couple whose son had been murdered. Brian and I looked at one another, and I said, "And so it begins."

We knew that at some point God would have some sort of ministry for us after we lost Victoria. He never wastes anything, and that includes the bad, as well as the good. Brian and I had shared with many of our friends how God was molding us to work for Him, and this was our first opportunity to share our journey with another family who was beginning the same walk.

> Blessed are those who mourn, for they will be comforted.
>
> Matthew 5:4 (NIV)

The look of utter pain was evident when we entered their home. We sat down and talked with these parents who were nearly drowning in pain and sadness. As we shared our story, I could see that they were very glad to have someone there who really *knew* what they were going through. Brian shared our journey with the promise that God can truly heal the brokenhearted. I shared about how He was helping us to cope with our loss and that He could help them as well. We spent about an hour with them, and then we left.

One thing that the mother shared with us was that they had donated several of their son's organs to help others. What a blessing that I could tell them that they had helped others to live, even though their son had died. About a year or so later, this couple answered a phone call from the man who received their son's heart. The two families met. It was wonderful that this family, who lost their son, could now see that he "lived on" in another person. The mother, who was a nurse, asked if she could feel the heartbeat of her son. The man was gracious and allowed her to do so. What a fabulous thing to happen! God is in charge of every moment of our lives and proved how He extends life sometimes, even through organ donations.

Several months later, while in church one Sunday, one of our friends told us of a couple in the church whose son was killed in a tragic accident in another state. As it so happened, that couple was in church that very morning. Brian and I made a beeline over to them. We were again able to share God's comfort and love with them. They were so happy to see someone who really knew their pain and suffering. We have kept in touch with this couple over the years, and they are doing well. The wife is actually helping out in a ministry of the church for people who have lost a loved one! Another praise!

We have also visited with a family whose eldest son was murdered on their front doorstep. It occurred at a party he was hosting. Some uninvited people showed up and started a fight. Their son was fatally stabbed. The family had actually been right inside the home at the time of the stabbing. How horrendous this was for them! We spent time with them and shared our story. As we left, we prayed for them to ask God for the comfort only He can give and to forge ahead with their lives, especially since they had other children in the household. We have seen the wife several times since then, and she has always expressed gratitude for our visit.

One of the best things that we can do is to share our experiences with others who may be going through similar circumstances. We are always willing to go and see families who allow us to come over, and we have been able to share our Lord Jesus with them all.

One day, Brian and I were on a long drive and stopped at a country bed and breakfast. While we were there, the owner came out, and we visited with her for a while. She shared that a family at her church had just lost their son, and she did not know how to minister to them. Brian and I shared our story, and she was so grateful to have someone tell her things she could do for the family during this time! See how God works? He will help and heal us all, if we allow Him to do so.

It Will Get Better, but It Will Never Be Okay

Leah

God is our refuge and strength, an ever-present help in trouble. Therefore we will not fear, though the earth give way and the mountains fall into the heart of the sea.

Psalm 46:1–2 (NASB)

When Brian and I go to visit with a family who has lost a child, invariably someone will ask us, "Does it ever get easier or better?" My answer is that yes, it will get better, but it will never be okay. The natural order of life is not for parents to outlive their children. We are to raise them and rejoice in their lives and accomplishments, not see those lives cut short before ours.

God has always been my great Comforter. This is what I can share with the families who are left behind. When Victoria died, I felt that my life had suddenly been slammed by a Mack truck going one hundred miles per hour. I was numb with shock, grief, and anger. I had been praying for a long time (nearly two years) that Victoria would return to God. I had placed expectations of just how God was supposed to answer my prayers. My prayers were very specific as I daily prayed, "Dear God, please take care of Victoria. Please bring her back to you, her first love, by whatever means needed. However, please spare her life so she can see all the wasted time away from you." Sounds pretty smug, right? I wanted her to return to God but only under my terms. Of course I was angry with God!

The wonderful thing, however, is that God already knew his plan for Victoria and for Brian and me. He tells us in the Bible:

> Do not fear those who kill the body but are unable to kill the soul; but rather fear Him who is able to destroy both soul and body in hell. Are not two sparrows sold for a cent? And yet not one of them will fall to the ground apart from your Father. But the very hairs of your head are all numbered.
>
> Matthew 10:28–30 (NASB)

In other words, God is concerned with even the smallest details of our lives!

The bottom line is this: Our God knows the number of days for our lives. He knows those who will serve Him and those who will not. He is the one who made us, and He loves us so! Victoria's days here on earth were eighteen years and four days—then He did answer my prayers. God brought her to be with Him in His time and in His way! I praise Him daily!

Grief for the loss of a loved one is different for each of us; however, we will all grieve. God is the Great

Provider (Jehovah Jireh) and the Great Physician (Jehovah Rapha) who can heal the body, as well as the soul. His presence is definitely a very present help in times of trouble.

One thing I would like to mention here is the pain. When we lost our daughter, both Brian and I had times (and still do) when the magnitude and pain of our loss threatened to overwhelm us. This is absolutely normal, and even though it is painful when it comes, the waves of sorrow and loss are actually a good thing—an important part of the healing process. We will always love and miss Victoria; however, we will not always have the overwhelming sorrow that we experienced during the first couple of years after her death. That is not to say that we have "gotten over it"—no way—it merely shows that we have gotten used to the "new normal"— what our lives are now. We are still parents, and that will never change; however, we also must continue our lives without our child.

When those emotions assail me, I spend time praying or just sitting quietly and allowing the emotions to wash over me. When those waves roll over me and I feel such pain now, I can actually let it come and remember the good things—not the loss. The times when we feel such sorrows are times when we need to be able to reach out to someone who can really understand and comfort us.

Another thing that I do is find Brian and talk with him about my feelings. Brian has learned to share his feelings more as well. When the two of us spend time recalling Victoria and her life, it helps both of us. A burden shared is no longer a burden. I believe that because of our talks and our long drives in the country,

Brian and I are much, much closer as husband and wife, as well as best friends. In my mind, the most important thing we can do for our spouses is love them and allow them to become our best friends. We are in this together, and it is so comforting to realize that we are not alone.

If you are not acquainted with the one who made you and knew you, even when you were within your mother's womb (Psalm 139:13–16), I offer you a chance to get to know him personally right now. Remember, God knows us inside and out!

If you believe in God, who created this earth and all that is in it, you can begin a real relationship with Him. When His creation, man, did not follow Him perfectly, those of us who were born afterward received a "curse of sin" on our lives. The only way to change that was for God to offer a true and complete sacrifice on our behalf.

That sacrifice was His only Son, Jesus. He died for all sin forever—that means yours and mine! All you or anyone else needs to do is acknowledge God's great sacrifice of his own Son and believe that Jesus was raised up from death to be with God. Then tell him so and ask for him to come into your heart and live within you.

Remember, God knows exactly what you are feeling as a parent who has lost a child—He lost one too! It is good to be able to talk with Him and to know the comfort that it brings.

I like to call my special times with God "parent-to-parent talks." Yes, I know that sounds odd to some people; however, when I need to speak things that are so painful and dear to my heart, who better to listen to me and love me than my heavenly Father? I have told

Him of my pain, my anger—every emotion that I felt and still feel at times. He understands them all. God has the wonderful ability to feel everything we feel, because He created us in his own image! I feel his presence when we talk to each other. Now when I hear God speak to me, it isn't necessarily an audible voice. He speaks to me through the peace in my heart, through my thoughts of His caring ways. He even sometimes sends yellow butterflies to let me know that He cares. Victoria and I both loved yellow butterflies so much— our favorite color! I believe that He shows us in many ways how much He loves us and wants to comfort us. All we need to do is share our innermost pain and feelings with Him.

> And without faith it is impossible to please Him, for he who comes to God must believe that He is and that He is a rewarder of those who seek Him.
>
> Hebrews 11:6 (NASB)

Helpful Hints
for Those Who
Want to Help

Leah

Friends love through all kinds of weather, and families stick together in all kinds of trouble.

Proverbs 17:17 (MSG)

When a loved one dies, no matter what the cause,
we feel the loss deeply, especially if that person was
a spouse, a close relative, or a friend. When a parent
loses their child, there is even more of a sense of loss
that covers not only the present but also the future. For
Brian and me, this loss was more than just the loss of
our only child—it meant the loss of any future grand-
children as well. The tender and loving care given to
us at that time was immeasurable. Friends, family, and
even strangers gathered around us and cared for us in
every way imaginable: spiritually, physically, and emotionally. It was the care, concern, and prayer support

shown by them that gave us the strength to let God comfort us—which he did—through their ministering hands and love.

If you know someone who has lost a loved one, no matter how they died, you may benefit from suggestions about how best to support them. What can you do to help, comfort, or counsel them? Below are some ideas that a dear friend and I have compiled from our experience. Diane and I spent many hours talking about what we thought others might wish to do for a grieving family. I have divided these suggestions into three categories: spiritual, physical, and emotional. My hope is that when someone you know loses a dear one, you will be better able to anticipate their needs and provide the loving care that is so necessary for them.

Spiritual

In the same way the Spirit also helps our weakness; for we do not know how to pray as we should, but the Spirit Himself intercedes for us with groanings too deep for words.

Romans 8:26 (NIV)

First, pray for them. No matter what their relationship is with God, they will need all the prayers you can pray for them.

If they are willing, pray with them. They may not be able to articulate their prayers, but be there to strengthen them if they wish to pray. Never try to force them to do so!

Be gentle with their feelings. Many people cannot understand why God would allow this to happen. Their emotions will run the gamut; they may be very angry or very sad at times.

Your "job" is to be ready at any moment to pray for them, to share God's comfort with them, and to be a source of strength in the midst of unimaginable pain. You can only do this with God's help. Ask him!

Physical

> In everything I did, I showed you that by this kind of hard work we must help the weak, remembering the words the Lord Jesus himself said: "It is more blessed to give than to receive."
>
> Acts 20:35 (NIV)

Bring food. Many folks like to bring food so that the family doesn't have to think about cooking. Be sure to put your name on the dish so that they may thank you later.

Bring a large ice chest filled with ice for water and soft drinks.

If you are at their home, make certain that every couple of hours or so they get something to eat, even if it's only a couple of bites. Shock and sorrow are a powerfully draining combination.

Make a list of all the food that comes in, along with the names of those who brought it. (So many people brought food to us, but nobody thought to make a list. Thus many people did not get a thank-you note from us!)

Ask them if you may help answer the phones, especially if it is a death resulting in media coverage. Once the news is known, many people will call the house to offer their condolences. The parents may not be able to talk on the phone. If there is someone answering the calls and writing down who called, the parents or other family members can return these calls when they are physically and emotionally capable.

If the family has not thought of it, suggest that they may wish to open a memorial fund in the child's name for people who may wish to donate to the family in lieu of flowers. Some people might not feel comfortable cooking something, sending flowers, or even visiting with the family. The opportunity to contribute to a memorial fund gives them a tangible way to help out, as well as to show the grieving family that they care. Sometimes the family has no life insurance on their children, and the financial burden of a funeral and burial can be daunting.

Bring the essentials: tissues, toilet paper, paper plates, plastic cups, napkins, paper towels, plastic forks, spoons and knives, and kitchen trash bags. There will be many people in and out of their house for several days, not to mention probable out-of-town guests, and most families do not have enough dishware/flatware to accommodate this many people. Not everyone has the emotional energy or the desire to wash dishes during this time.

If you are a close friend and no one has thought to ask, volunteer to accompany them to make funeral arrangements. Usually this will be something the family will want to handle, but it doesn't hurt for you to be with them in a support capacity when they actually make the arrangements.

You might consider helping clean up the kitchen or straighten around the house when people leave.

Do not disappear in the days after the service. When the funeral is over, the grief does not end for the family. From having days of initial shock, grief, sadness, and often-unmanageable swirling activity, the transition to reality and silence after the service may be emotionally painful.

Do not make empty promises. If you have made an offer to take the grieving couple to dinner or to just spend time with them, please follow through with your invitation. They will remember your promises to them.

Stay in touch. Try not to avoid the family members in weeks and months to come when you see them out in public by assuming that you are inadequate with your words. You just might be a blessing to them and be the recipient of a blessing for yourself. Jesus went to the brokenhearted and the sick; He knew they might have no hope and be a mess, but He went to them anyway to bless them and to minister to them. Be the hands and feet of our Lord and speak to those who are grieving. Remember, their grief did not end at the conclusion of the funeral service—it is ongoing. Be there for the grieving.

Emotional

I will lift up my eyes to the mountains; from where shall my help come? My help comes from the LORD, Who made heaven and earth.

Psalm 121:1–2 (NASB)

Blessed are those who mourn, for they shall be comforted.

Matthew 5:4 (NASB)

Be available. Be a caring servant and a quiet listener. This may mean not saying anything, just listening. The most intimate thing you can do with them is to sit with them as they pray, cry, scream, or talk. My dear accountability partner, Holly, came that first night and just sat next to me. She did not speak a single word. Her hand was on my knee, and she just sat there (praying silently, I'm sure!). Her availability was so very comforting to me; I'll never, ever forget her caring presence! Some of the most comforting times and touching moments occurred when Victoria's friends came to the house and just sat in front of me on the floor. Many were tearful, but all were there to offer us support and to mourn with us. They merely sat there; no one tried to carry on much of a conversation at all.

Don't be afraid to let the family talk about their child. This can be very healing. Talk about things you remember about their child. Parents want others to remember, even if it is hard.

Speak the child's name when talking about him or her. As parents, much thought usually goes into naming our children, and it is comforting to know others remember that they lived.

Tell them if you think of their child and what you remember about them. Did they make a difference in your life or teach you something? If so, please tell them.

Please be understanding about the parents' needing to excuse themselves, no matter what the reason. For instance, since our daughter was a murder victim, the sheriffs visited us for several days as they followed up leads. Brian and I constantly had to excuse ourselves and go talk with them. There are also some moments when the parents want to be alone for a short time.

I am certain that there are many other things you can offer to do. These are just a few of the things that we remembered, things we would not have thought of otherwise. Being available, loving, kind, and helpful are the best things to do to show your care and love.

The Journey
Continues ...

Brian

No temptation has overtaken you but such as is
common to man; and God is faithful, who will not
allow you to be tempted beyond what you are able,
but with the temptation will provide the way of
escape also, so that you will be able to endure it.

1 Corinthians 10:13 (NASB)

There is an old saying in life: It's not about the distance;
it's about the journey. When we walk through life, we
all have a tendency to get caught up in the daily routine
of life: the "grind," the "stuff," or, better yet, the "job."
You will hear people say, "This is what I do," or, better
yet, "This is my destiny or karma."

Life can be dull at times, and at other times, it seems
to run so fast that we can barely keep our heads above
water and find little time to take a deep breath. For
others, this life can be a time of rushing from sunrise to
sunset, or it can be one of that dreaded word—*drama*!

The kind of drama that I am talking about starts before we first wake up. It drags you out of the bed, keeps you from your appointed tasks and goals for the day, and changes your mood on the slightest word, grunt, or look.

For Leah and me, drama days would start first thing in the morning. *Do we really want to get out of bed now? Do we really want to face the world today? Lord, is this a dream? We just cannot believe this is happening to us! It's not fair!* My mother used to have a saying when we would scream about things in life and yell, "It's not fair!" She would tell me, "Brian, we are on the planet Earth, not the planet Not Fair."

Mom's words certainly cut to the chase, didn't they? Life went on, and so did we. We did not enter this world with a manual on what to do next or how to handle this deep, hurting pain of the loss of our only child. But one thing did prevail: We found comfort by remembering God's Word. We were reminded daily that God is God, He still loved us, and His Word said that He would never leave us or forsake us.

> Let your conduct be without covetousness; be content with such things as you have. For He Himself has said, "I will never leave you nor forsake you."
>
> Hebrews 13:5 (KJV)

Sometimes we get so caught up in the trivial things of life, dwell on the darkest parts, and forget that we have a loving God who is always there to help us. I have shared on one or more occasions with people that God never shuts a door unless He opens a window. He will always give us an escape route from our heaviest challenges in life. His great promise for this is found in Psalms.

> As for me, I will call upon God, and the LORD shall save me. Evening and morning and at noon I will pray, and cry aloud, and He shall hear my voice. He has redeemed my soul in peace from the battle that was against me, for there were many against me.
>
> Psalm 55:16–18 (NKJV)

We began to live our lives one day at a time, for we did not know what tomorrow would bring. We learned to take baby steps to get from point A to point B. But most importantly, we needed God's help—the kind of help that only He could send us. Praise God that we were beneficiaries of that help from the Lord.

At first, the immediate help came from an outpouring of love and assistance from our small group Bible study and church family. Then, as each new day dawned, the help continued through friends, neighbors, and those we had known from previous churches. We are not high-profile people. Our faces are not on the cover of any magazines, advertisements, or local papers. Neither one of us has been seen on television or had our names and faces plastered on the Internet. We are just common, ordinary folk. Just like you. And yet God loved us so much that He answered our cries and prayers for help and sent us help from near and afar.

So you may be asking yourself, "What am I to do?"

We found that, instead of reaching inward to ourselves, we needed to reach outward. Yes, outward! First to God for His love, His grace, and His understanding. Remember, He too lost a son. Then we reached out to our family and friends, our local church, and professionals for help. Yes, I am suggesting that you seek professional help. Seek someone who has been through the fire before you. Seek someone who has lived and survived the hard trials in life.

God will take our pains, losses, and failures and reshape them to be used by Him to be a blessing for someone else in your future. He has given us a promise to be there for us and gives us a vision for the future, if we ask Him.

> This is my command—be strong and courageous!
> Do not be afraid or discouraged. For the Lord your
> God is with you wherever you go.
>
> Joshua 1:9 (NLT)

How cool is that? We do not have to be afraid or to fear today or tomorrow, because He is with us every step of the way. Not maybe, if He has time and can fit it into his schedule. Not after He is finished with the next set of problems from His other children, and not tomorrow.

When we opened ourselves to be obedient, willing, and able, God gave us the strength that we needed to make it through each day. He gave us an opportunity to share our loss in such a way that it blessed others. Our story helped those who were struggling with their own loss, whether it was a child, husband, loved one, job, or career—anything or anyone who was very close to them.

So how does the journey continue? For us, it has been an exciting discovery of divine intersections on a daily basis. We are no longer surprised when a special

God-moment presents itself. It may come in a phone call from someone we know or a perfect stranger. It can occur at the bank, grocery store, vet clinic, or mall—the opportunities are endless. Merely being open to listening to people, and having a sense of compassion and caring, causes others to open up to us and share what is heavy on their hearts.

We have all been called to minister to one another, to lift up, edify, and to encourage one another. Our focus is not on ourselves but on others and on how we can help them. When there is less of me, there is more of thee.

> We have also a more sure word of prophecy; where-unto ye do well that ye take heed, as unto a light that shineth in a dark place, until the day dawn, and the day star arise in your hearts.
>
> 2 Peter 1:19 (KJV)

We are to let our light shine so that others will come close to see what is different about us. While we were searching for comfort, we found that comfort in our Savior's arms, and he led us out of the darkness and into the light. From his arms, we have been blessed to help others who are struggling with their loss and pain. We have shared with them that there is hope and that the light at the end of the tunnel is not a train coming, but the cross, the true light—the Way.

> Then Jesus again spoke to them, saying, "I am the Light of the world; he who follows Me will not walk in the darkness, but will have the Light of life."
>
> John 8:12 (NASB)

There is something exciting about driving through the countryside. There seems to be something different at every turn, and we really have to focus on what is coming next. When we get on a freeway, we are focused on the traffic around us, and we put our blinders on—all we see is the road and those around us. The path is filled with nothing more and nothing less, just road and white lines.

But when we get off the main highway and begin to relax, we can then take in all of the splendor and beauty that the Lord has made. This is how He wants us to live our lives: to be ready for the open road, to breathe in all that He has for us, and to share the splendor of who He is as we feel the warmth of His embrace.

The journey continues. We have learned to let go and let God direct our every step.

> For I consider that the sufferings of this present time are not worthy to be compared with the glory that is to be revealed to us.
>
> Romans 8:18 (NASB)

listen|imagine|view|experience

AUDIO BOOK DOWNLOAD INCLUDED WITH THIS BOOK!

In your hands you hold a complete digital entertainment package. In addition to the paper version, you receive a free download of the audio version of this book. Simply use the code listed below when visiting our website. Once downloaded to your computer, you can listen to the book through your computer's speakers, burn it to an audio CD or save the file to your portable music device (such as Apple's popular iPod) and listen on the go!

How to get your free audio book digital download:

1. Visit www.tatepublishing.com and click on the e|LIVE logo on the home page.
2. Enter the following coupon code:
   4b63-4cb1-5c20-74e5-ca66-51dc-d403-954f
3. Download the audio book from your e|LIVE digital locker and begin enjoying your new digital entertainment package today!